# TO HAVE A GRAVEYARD AS A FRIEND

In Mortis Veritas

## True stories told by those inside the caskets

By Michael Pace

ISBN-13: 978-1523833696
ISBN-10: 1523833696

First Edition, January 2016

Published by
*Groundwaters* Publishing, LLC

P.O. Box 50, Lorane, Oregon 97451
http://www.groundwaterspublishing.com

Introduction:

# *Actus Orsus Ultimus Est*
## (The beginning of the Final Act)

I am Michael.

I have been inspired by the expired, so to speak.

The inspiration for this book began as a small seed planted by a random occurrence that I witnessed when I was about 19. (I am in my sixties at the time of this writing). All in this book that lies ahead for you has happened to me. It is all true. But like the announcer for the "Dragnet" show from the late 1960s was fond of saying, "Only the names have been changed to protect the innocent."

In my late teens, I had a part-time job working at a funeral home, mainly transporting the deceased, doing odd jobs around the grounds, and other duties.

One day a co-worker and I were tasked with taking cremains, (the result of a cremation) from a city in Southern California to another city two hundred miles north for placement in a mausoleum. This was not an infrequent occurrence...as families moved, so did the remains of their deceased relatives.

We arrived at our destination and dutifully placed the container in its appointed niche. My partner walked away, but I lingered for a bit.

Off to one side of me I heard a raspy voice talking in low tones. I could not make out the words. I turned my head to catch a glimpse of the speaker, yet not wanting to disturb his tranquility.

I was stunned and thrilled! The voice belonged to George Burns, and he was talking to Gracie, his wife who had preceded him in death, at that time, by ten years. I moved gingerly ever closer to only catch snippets of a very private conversation.

"...Tootsie" (his dog) "had her nails clipped today, you know how she hates that..."

"Tomorrow Lionel will be taking me to the club to play bridge. Any message I should take to the boys?" (His other playing partners)

George Burns! Talking to his deceased wife! Was he a senile old man? Of course not. People have been talking to their dead friends and relatives since the dawn of time. It gives them comfort and allows them to reflect...if but for a moment...peaceful memories. It is a time for their soul to connect with the soul of their beloved.

Perhaps the departed person "talks" back, perhaps not. Who are we to say, until it is us sitting at that spot?

Years later as a licensed funeral director I would remember that day. I was forced along my journey to deconstruct my life and to reconstruct it. I had tough lessons to learn along the way.

Spending many hours every week amongst the dead had very little impact on me, a cold callous young man who knew it all. Then one day my boss challenged me to find meaning in my job, and perhaps find a purpose for my life. He suggested I look deeper into the lives of the people I was burying.

Could the very dead help even me?

If I "listened" to them through the files we kept, would they "talk" to me? Could I learn of their successes and failures? More importantly, would I apply what I learned?

Read our adventures. See what you think.

# Acknowledgments

I can take very little credit for this book. Love and thanks go out to many people, and I'm sure I will forget some.

- Mr. and Mrs. Samuel Cruz Sr. housed and fed me as a teenager when I found myself in dire straits. I worked hard at minimum wage jobs and fell short on the rent often, but still they kept me as one of their own.

- Dr. Clifford Comisky helped me with the initial editing of the book.

- My daughter Natalie, who you will soon meet, a woman beautiful in person and in spirit.

- Andrea, my wife, my love and inspiration, who you will meet her in this book. She is everything and more than you will read on these pages... patient, kind, and stern when necessary.

In my profession, I have witnessed many times the deep, deep love of couples that can almost be excruciating... so much so that upon the death of one, the grief is almost palpable. You will witness that first hand, also, as they talk to their deceased loved one.

I do not look forward to whatever scenario awaits Andrea and me. The only way that we can mitigate the inevitable is to love each other every day. Time is short and is moving faster.

- Lastly, but most important, I give thanks to my God, eternal, not created, who confounds the wise and lifts up the foolish. It is because of my God that I've been offered a second (and third and fourth) chance to be here.

Should I gain any praise, let it go to Calvary.

# Table of Contents

# Chapter 1:
# Death in a Mirror

A t the age of 26, I turned my thoughts to the ultimate of human experience, that of death. I chose to become a licensed funeral director. It seemed like the perfect segue in the life of a man who had just completed a military career as a Navy Pharmacist's Mate, thrust unwillingly into the Hell of the Korean War. There I was introduced to death, tasted death, fought with death. It was the enemy, to be feared, despised and avoided at all costs. But avoiding it was not a luxury I would be afforded. War time medicine was not so much a practice as it was a postponement of the inevitable.

It was the loss of limbs, the loss of function and the loss of hope that was seen in vacant stares. It was living, if you wished to call it that, with a mind moving rapidly, sending signals to a body that could not respond. I grieved at the loss of the physical life, but many times felt relief. Prolonging a man's pain and suffering was, in my opinion at that time, cruel and unjust. I would not have wished that promise of a tortured future on a wounded animal.

Perhaps I became somewhat immune – hardened – to death and suffering,

It has been said that death is the one experience we are closest to, but one we will never know, because we cannot experience it . It is something – a feeling – that all mankind shares equally. It is only confronted when we must, and for the most part, we are ill-prepared.

Marching off to Korea, I didn't give it too much thought. Death came to other people, certainly not to me. I was the typical invincible youth – bold, brash and quick to make my opinions known. Usually they were wrong at best, hurtful at worst, and always spoken at the most insensitive moment.

The hurtful part went both ways. I am sporting two fewer teeth as a reward for voicing my opinions, and a nose broken four times. I sustained a fracture over my right eye, and all this before I turned thirty. These wounds were received, shall we say, as the result of "friendly fire." For the most part, I left Korea fairly unscathed, at least from combat.

I am 87 now. I look back on one life. Those who met me after I turned 60 might say I am level-headed, slow to anger, and a good source for sound advice.

"Thanks," I say, but I had a little help.

What causes a narcissistic, egocentric, know-it-all youngster to start thinking about someone, something, other than his own self and self-interests? Was it numerous brushes with death?

Nah. Death had become just another friendly element to me.

Was it being surrounded by quality friends who forced him to look at life in a mature manner?

Nope. I would not develop close friendships until I was in my thirties.

Was it a girl?

Well... partly. I met my wife of 50 years through one of my friends to whom I will introduce you later.

Divine intervention? More than likely, although I did not know it or acknowledge it at the time.

Learning to respect and value other people was a combination of all the above, mixed over a long, long time. It had to be learned through bitter experience. Common sense, morality, and human bonding cannot be legislated.

I have had the privilege of mentoring younger people. A few have told me they wish to be like me. I give them this old adage: "One thing you can be sure of... if you ever see a turtle on a fence post. He had a lot of help getting there."

Mentoring can be quite nerve-wracking. It has been said "Show me your mentors and I will show you yourself in future years."

Do I really want to see myself in others?

I had a lot of help getting here from some very unlikely sources. Ed, my boss at the funeral home who had ample reason to fire me many times over, must have seen a broken spirit that was worth repairing. He kept me employed at the same place until he died. By then, I was so ensconced, and so content, I knew I would never leave.

My wife was the same; sticking by me when a lesser mortal would have thrown up her hands in dismay and walked away.

What completed me was learning the secrets of the dead, from the dead... literally. Through the files we kept, it was as if they talked with me. The more I read, the more they showed me. Their sorrow and shame, joy and victory... The Path. The Way.

When I was selfish, they taught me to share. When I leaned heavily on my own talents, they showed me my glaring weaknesses. When I exhibited seething hatred for my fellow man, they held up a mirror. I was taught by reading of the plight of one of them that I couldn't feel love and give respect until I learned to respect myself; not in a haughty, self-serving way, but to be content with the individual that the Creator put in front of that mirror.

Korea had taught me to fear and loathe death. My friends taught me that a life worth living ends in a death with meaning. The death of the common man is a heroic deed. His life, full of regrets, mistakes, and successes can be taken and learned from. It is a lifetime of learning. The beautiful lives of many that transformed me from a discontented self-serving man of no hope and of no value to anyone to a man that can pass life lessons, full of substance, to others (I can't wait to have you meet my friend Henny Kaiser!)... If we would only listen.

Initially I thought I would write about the philosophy of death so I could leave something for my children. I would write about my feelings, my personal thoughts. But as I sat down to write, I realized I was getting in over my head. Death was too metaphysical, too abstract.

*Hmmm..,* I thought. *Perhaps it is a topic best left to doctors or ministers.*

I was sharing my dilemma and my desire to write with my friend, mentor, and employer of many years, Ed Carson. A few days later he told me he had an answer. He took me to his office and with a sweeping flair of his arm, opened up his file cabinet filled with cases he had done over the years. I stared into it. No bells rang.

"Think, man!" he said. "Here are your heroes. Here are your teachers. They are the uncelebrated, the ordinary. Let them recount, in their own words, the lives lived, the eras and the environment in which they had to survive. What tough lessons did they learn? Indeed. Were they astute enough to learn them or continue to fail? How did it feel to be a certain person in a certain time and place? What made them who they were? Did we bury or cremate anybody mediocre?"

*Hmmm.* Now here was a tangible challenge I could handle, and one that someone might actually get something out of! I could write of the dead. The good, the bad and the gruesome. Those who would come after me could learn from the mistakes of the dead. Words would come easy. My dead friends had nothing else better to do with their time than to wax eloquent with words of life. I knew these people! They were seemingly inarticulate and unable to speak, but when I stooped low and took the time to listen, I savored their beautiful words like fine wine.

The result? You'll see. At times, I think they were as astonished as I was. A case in point: Irma and Roger Glendale.

Irma died several years after her husband. He lived his last years lost in the fog of Alzheimer's; she died in a nice home with all her mental faculties intact. In her final days, we laughed together. She taught me to look out on the city at night. Look at all the lights. Perhaps at a death, one of those lights would go out.

At times she and I would name some of those lights. I named mine Despair, Dismal, and Hopeless. I looked at this beautiful lady and saw nothing in her present state that I thought would be worth clinging to had I been in her place, but she surprised me by naming her lights Hope, Faith and Comfort. She tried at the time to convince me that she had everything to live for, and dying, she would gain even more. But, I was not at the point in my life where I cared to listen. Perhaps you will meet the Glendales later and I will let her tell the story in her own words.

As I recount the stories of the dead, as they were told to me, you may be astonished to discover we, the living, reflect on death a lot. Once my dead friends began to speak, they didn't want to stop. They offered all sorts of opinions; some put forth a challenge.

Those that had faith had an easier time leaving. For some, even now, I wonder, "Are they at peace?"

By the way, I met Adelina, my wife of 50 years, through Irma Glendale. To be perfectly candid, being surrounded by death almost daily did nothing to ease the pain of Adelina's passing, but we still talk. I know she is beckoning because she is fearful for my soul… or so she told me numerous times when she was with me in body. Ironically, it has only been in the past few years that I have been convinced that where she is, I stand a good chance of being there as well. It took a mixture of faith and  assurance from my wife and others who went on ahead. Still, I am a bit nervous and frightened, although at least now I am cautiously optimistic.

Anyway, my kids (Kids! Hah! They are over 50 now!) know I dwell on these things at times, and in their own way they try to console me. "Who would want to live to be 90?" they chide.

It was said that Winston Churchill was asked that very question. He was rumored to have responded, "Those who are 89."

Both my children pursued careers outside the funeral profession and I am proud that they are fully equipped to withstand or to enjoy, all that the world has to send their way. They have lots of quality people in their lives. Unlike their father, they listen.

So come with me on my journey. Come as we greet my company. Understand why the graveyard is my friend.

I am retired, glad to be writing this, and generally looking forward to whatever happens.

Don't get me wrong. I am just as nervous about facing the challenge of death as the next person, as perhaps, you are. But please, at least listen. I was guilty of not listening. You see, my first dead friend, Mr. Gail Thomas, was almost my last.

# Chapter 2:
# Fools Rush In

Following my job interview, this brash, twenty-two year-old walked out of Carson's funeral home with less confidence than when I walked in. The interview had taken me by surprise. Considering the time and preparation I had spent in conjuring up bizarre scenarios in my head and mulling over intelligent-sounding responses to likely questions, I was a bit shocked when Ed, my prospective boss stood up fifteen minutes into the interview and offered me his hand.

"Well, Son," he said with what I would soon realize was his trademarked grin, "the job is yours if you want it. Can you start Monday?"

I rose hesitantly and took the proffered hand. "Sure," I responded, my hesitation hiding my surprise.

I managed to shuffle out the door, somewhat dismayed. He had not given me the opportunity to dazzle him with my sharp, keen insight that would convince him I was more mature than my years.

Still desiring to make a good first impression, I arrived at work fifteen minutes early on my first day. Much to my dismay the place was already bustling with activity. Then I remembered. Death is a twenty-four-hour business.

Ed greeted me with an outstretched hand and a smile; however, I was not in such an expansive mood.

"Hi, Michael," he beamed, much too cheery for me this early in the morning. "Let's take a quick tour. I don't have much work for you just yet but not to worry, it will come soon enough."

The facilities were small and dated, but functional. This was certainly not what I had been accustomed to for the last two years as a student, having been taught at one of the largest and finest equipped mortuary schools in the West.

No matter. With my training, I would most assuredly rise to the top here quickly and teach my new colleagues the latest and greatest techniques which I was privy to. I would have no problem with job security and, because of my innovations, business would skyrocket.

The tour over, we walked to the sparsely furnished main office and met with a secretary whose name was Donna, I think. I was introduced to other staff as they passed by. I glanced at them, but took no interest in remembering their names or faces. Ed had me fill out the requisite new-hire forms, and then assigned me a mentor for the rest of the day.

Although my mentor was pleasant and professional, I sensed his attitude toward the deceased clientele was much like that found in real estate; grab them first when you can in order to earn your commission.

Days later, I realized he must have sensed my hostility. When I told him bluntly of my perception, he bristled; his body language indicating a readiness for physical confrontation, if necessary. "Ed does not run his place like that. He assigns cases to the directors he feels can best tailor their talents to the client's needs, and he is good at it. You should only wish that you could be half as astute as he is."

He was almost hissing through clenched teeth now. "We are all salaried." He turned on his heels and left.

In my blindness as a youth I figured he was hostile because I was so young and confident; perhaps he was intimidated by my education. I was somewhat surprised that he was waiting for me the following day, smiling, apparently willing to continue mentoring me.

Several days later, we were in deep concentration, dealing with a decedent, when Ed broke in and motioned to me. I felt a sense of foreboding; bile quickly rose from my stomach. I followed him into his office and he handed me a file. I stared at the cover numbly, not wishing to know its contents.

"Well, it looks like we might have found a client for you. Tomorrow you will meet Mr. Gail Thomas."

I looked at him, my expression one of questioning mixed with a bit of relief. His smile indicated we were through, and there was nothing more he had to offer. If he knew of the earlier confrontation with my mentor, he never mentioned it. I left with the file and found an empty desk in the prep room to study the details. Here was my chance! My first solo case! I would pore over the papers and know all about the man before I met him. I would present myself in the appropriate attire and show these people what a man in this profession, recently graduated, could do!

The following day I pulled into my parking place early, and for the first time since I hired on, noticed the sign: "For Employees Only." I exited my car with a sense of newfound ownership, assured in the knowledge that I would grab this job by the tail. I was upbeat and confident. I had gone to great lengths to choose my suit and tie. I was early and Mr. Thomas was not quite ready for me. I paced about, ready to jump when the word was given.

Finally! Time to meet my first client and begin building lasting relationships.

Mr. Thomas had a casual appearance. He was dressed in a red flannel, long-sleeve shirt, denim jeans and brown heavy-soled shoes. He was almost seventy years old, but still had thick black hair, streaked with just the right amount of gray. He was well-tanned, and from what I remembered from his file, had been a rancher. He certainly looked like a "man's man."

I walked over to where he lay.

"Glad to meet you, Mr. Thomas," I said with relish. One always remembers their first dollar, their first car… and their first corpse. Mr. Thomas was my very first solo case since graduating from school and completing all requirements for both licenses a funeral director must carry – administrative, and the Certificate of Embalming. He was to be my proving ground. I would not fail.

There was an envelope crammed into a shirt pocket addressed to the funeral home. I opened it to find some handwritten instructions from his wife. I gave the contents a cursory glance and flipped it aside.

Mrs. Thomas had opted for a private viewing rather than direct cremation. Viewing would be by invitation only, with very few visitors other than the immediate family.

Now that I had acquainted myself with the man, it was time to briefly get acquainted with the family. Mrs. Thomas was already in Ed's office. I would meet the son later.

I introduced myself using my best "stage" voice; she looked up at me with what seemed to be a sense of apprehension, but I was too immersed in myself to take much notice.

She took a deep breath and her shoulders seemed to relax a bit as she began to tell me about her husband. "He was a rancher most of his life; a real outdoorsman. I gave him a son, who is still working the ranch. Gail was a proud, self-sufficient man."

She put a hand lightly on my arm, and then looked at Ed, almost in a panic. She sat down and began to weep quietly. I took that as my cue to leave. I still had not mastered the emotional part of the job. I hoped that Ed would sit with her and say all the right words.

Walking across the asphalt to the work area, I paused when I heard hurried footsteps behind me. It was Ed. "A word of advice," he cautioned, "Remember why you came into this profession." Then he was gone.

I entered the preparation room which housed the exam table and the crematory to begin Mr. Thomas' transformation, having no idea what Ed meant.

Even dead, Mr. Thomas seemed to be in his prime; a solid strapping man. The skin on his face and hands showed the deep tan and harsh furrows that come from braving the elements. He proved to be a splendid specimen for my first case, all the easier for a very nice presentation. He looked like he would have been quite comfortable stepping out of an Old West novel. I took great pains in applying just the right colors to his face. I worked his hair neatly, even adding a bit of dye to offset the gray. His current attire would have to go. I wasn't going to show off my handiwork on a man in blue denim jeans, boots, and a thick work shirt. I picked out a dress shirt, tie, and coat that fit him, suitable for the viewing. The funeral home would get it back before cremation. Most funeral homes kept an array of clothes available for situations such as this.

In funeral parlance, what I was doing was "setting the features." I set Mr. Thomas' mouth lifelike; even adding a touch of balm to give his lips moisture and color. Then I rubbed a special astringent into the loose folds under his eyes to restore a few years, and temper the effects of sun damage. The fingers I interlaced in a gesture of reflective repose. I made sure to remember the dashes of strategically-placed scented talc.

The preparation took several hours and I checked and rechecked my work. Ed came in a time or two and shook his head, smiling, but only managed to say "Uh huh, uh huh."

When I was actively working, it had always been my habit to review cases the night before the burial, cremation or whatever. I wanted to be prepared, even for last minute changes the family might have, if any. I needed to know the family, know the decedent. Mulling over a pending case usually took place in my study, at night, or perhaps sitting in front of the crematory for the three hours it took for the process.

Because he was my first case, I remembered all the details. I vividly remember pausing to put myself in Mr. Thomas' place. What would he want ?How could I prepare him to aptly reflect the character of this rugged farming man? My instincts were clear on what he thought Mrs. Thomas and his boy would want to see as they bid him goodbye. He was looking at me from the preparation table and it was eerie how I could almost sense him wanting to meet his wife's expectations during her time of grief; to let her know he was at peace, so she could be at peace.

I listened to my instincts carefully. Problem was, I really didn't care. This was to be MY showcase. Any amateur could throw some jeans and a flannel shirt on a corpse.

The following day, Mrs. Carson arrived, accompanied by her son. The rough life showed on the face of the woman; small but hard. The son was big and sturdy. I escorted them respectfully to the viewing room then stood quietly outside the door awaiting any last minute wishes or whims. I had great expectations. I would linger about, not waiting for a compliment, but… well… maybe just a little one. However, I could certainly act gracious and humble if necessary.

Often as is to be expected in these circumstances, I could hear muffled sobs through the door. Death is the Great Equalizer and moves the strong and the weak, intelligent and unschooled, to tears. The two exited the viewing room. The wife looked up at me and asked through her sobs, "Who took care of him?"

I bent my head in what I hoped to be a reverent pose and said, "I did," and like an expectant child, waited for the kudos I knew were coming.

Shaking her finger at me just inches from my nose and eyes blazing, she became furious, all hint of sorrow gone from her voice. "Well, young man, you made him look like a pansy! That… thing… in there is not my husband. He would strangle you with his bare hands if he could see himself."

Her eyes narrowed. She was an angry alley cat with claws extended, poised for the kill. "I just knew this was not Ed's work. My man would have been comfortable tending bar in an old saloon. You made him look like one of the barmaids. You should be ashamed. And those clothes! And that smell! Did you even take the time to read what was in the envelope?"

I took a step back, too shocked to speak, and tried to shrink away as she reached for her son's arm. They stomped out. From out of nowhere, Ed appeared. That man popped up everywhere. As always, he wore that strange-yet-knowing smile. He must have noticed my anger, that I was visibly shaken. "I got some coffee in the office," he said. "You want some?"

"No thanks," I hissed through gritted teeth. "There will be others. How ungrateful! Did you see the work I did?"

"Oh yes," he said, all hint of a smile gone. "I saw the work *you* did. I saw the work you did for *yourself*, not for your client." He punctuated his words. "You must get to know your clients, dead or alive. And remember... they are not dead until the family says they're dead. Mrs. Thomas cannot let her man go until she feels he is at peace. In the minds of the mourning family, a loved one is still alive until they let him go. She wants to remember him as he was the last time she saw him. Your job is to realize that the family never forgets the passage of a loved one. We are here to help them through the transition."

With that he shook his head and left me alone with my thoughts.

I remained angry the rest of the day. I let my bitterness fester as I prepared Mr. Thomas for cremation. I slammed drawers, I threw instruments. How crass! There was not one aspect of the preparation that Mrs. Thomas, or Ed, for that matter, seemed to appreciate! I felt as if all my work had gone for nothing, which only served to irritate me further.

*Remember why I came into this profession indeed!* My thoughts seemed so loud I felt the whole office could hear.

*Hey, all! I came into this profession because it suited my personality! I am not that person you run to when you have problems. Find someone else who will listen, who has sympathy. I care, but only about my own problems.*

I punched the keys to program the crematorium. Three hours later when all that had been Mr. Thomas was but a memory, I was still angry.

Sixty years later I remember, and I shudder, because I could almost hear Mr. Thomas as the flames danced about him, laughing at me, content with himself, but saying, *I told you so!*

11

# Chapter 3:
# The Howling Man

I spent a lot of time over the next few weeks looking over my shoulder. I just knew the staff was laughing behind my back. Why Ed was torturing me and not firing me was anybody's guess. Perhaps he enjoyed seeing me wallowing in my misery.

I was on my own now, tending to the wishes of many clients, all wanting cremation. I was bored. I was anxiously awaiting an interment, and it was difficult watching the other directors handling burials and church services.

Over time my bitterness softened, and I forced myself to be polite to all, but the mundane was not why I had entered the profession. Months after the Thomas incident, I had pretty much convinced myself that Ed was not going to fire me; perhaps just keep me around to pick up the dregs that no one else really wanted. And so it was for almost a year.

One day Ed called me to the office. He had another file folder in his hand. Perhaps, I thought, this was it! A service and interment!

I left the office with the file and went into the prep room to read it. I looked at the first and slammed the file to the desk. Another cremation! My disgust must have shown, because the omnipresent Ed appeared from out of 'who knows where.' If he had seen me slam the file down, he gave no indication. He leaned against the desk and flipped thorough the records.

"I got a call from the jail today. As soon as this fellow comes, he can be cremated. No viewing, no prep, nothing. All the papers are in order. This man was not a criminal. They put him in a holding cell because they had nowhere else to turn. He had some real bad mental health issues and his last days were quite intriguing. This city does not have an acute mental health facility. You might be interested to know he was the author of several books... a brilliant, brilliant man. As far as his family goes, no one is showing any interest in the proceedings.

"Now let's get to the important issue. You are asking yourself, 'Why did I single out this case to give to you, yet another routine cremation?'"

I remember saying something like, *Well, it had crossed my mind...*

Ed looked at me and there was urgency in his voice. "Look, Son. You're not going to last here or anywhere else for any length of time if you do not find purpose for your work. I know you know how to do your job. You are quite good. No. You need to ask yourself, 'Why?' Don't go wandering from job to job never knowing the 'why.'

"Sometimes, if I think it appropriate, I match my directors with cases. This case is going to give you an opportunity to answer some questions that, if I'm not mistaken, you're wrestling with. You have a choice with this man. Cremate him right away and be done with it, or dig into his past. Learn about him and learn from him. My directors have been here for years. They get to know many of their clients. If you find out about your man here, I think your outlook will change."

I chewed on the end of my pen as Ed rambled on. I could not bear to look him in the eye. I made a pretense of writing notes. He finally left and I resolved to cremate this guy as fast as I could and go home and lick my wounds yet again. I figured if I got home before dark I could polish up my résumé and start the job hunting process the next morning.

When Dr. Paul Anderson finally arrived, I could hardly believe the entity before me had at one time been human. He had not been in an accident, nor had he succumbed to a crippling disease. His arms and legs were intertwined in an inextricable mess. The stiffness of rigor mortis in death comes and goes, and afterwards the limbs are flaccid. But although rigor had long since passed, I could not budge his extremities. He looked, literally, like a pretzel.

I stood staring for the longest time. The death certificate was in my hand and I was faced with some decisions to make. How easy it would have been to cremate him and call it good. But I knew Ed had given me this man for a reason. I made up my mind. I would research the life of Paul Anderson before I consigned him to the flames.

I put the twisted man away for a time, but I could not will his image from my mind. Perhaps rigor had indeed locked Dr. Anderson's limbs in place. His knees were drawn up under his chin, contracted forever. His arms were crossed over his chest and his hands were clutching his knees. Even in death his eyes were ablaze in fear and torment. It was impossible to keep them closed. His mouth was locked open and contorted in fear. His cremation could wait.

I searched the courthouse for old records. The jail released what they had. Ed had told me Dr. Anderson was an author, so I went to the library to browse through some of his works. Could I gain any insight there?

I remember this because it was strange, having to do so much footwork for a simple cremation. This was long before the computer and the internet. Today when I talk to my kids about slide rules and card catalogues at the libraries; it has much the same effect as talking about ancient ruins!

I was genuinely shocked and dismayed to learn he was a preacher. I thought that preachers had all the answers, and they looked forward to death; welcomed it in fact. I expected all staunch church-goers to die with smiles on their faces, but a man who died like this? – having multiple degrees in church-related matters? This only served to foster my distrust of organized religions. After all, if they couldn't take hold of their own lives, how could they help us common folk?

Three days later, I beheld the man once again. I knew him now. I had studied his life. When I took him out of the cooler, I looked at Dr. Anderson a bit differently and he did not look like the same man. I marveled at the transformation in him.

I had been at the job for over a year by that time, but I can't remember. *Was Paul Anderson the one who changed? Or was it the beginning of a change in the way I viewed others? – myself?*

Usually Ed sought me out, but at closing time this particular day I sought him out.

"Hey, Ed," I began, a bit more contrite than was my custom, 'I am ready to cremate Dr. Anderson.'

"Good. Have a seat here. I think some fresh coffee is almost ready."

There were two chairs in the office, but we didn't use them. Dr. Anderson and Ed were my audience, but I was not in the mood to wax eloquent or boast. I had taken extensive notes which I held, but on second thought I put them down.

I let out a big sigh, shook my head in dismay, and began the story.

"Dr. Paul Anderson was set to be a gifted orator from an early age. He had a beautiful speaking voice. You wouldn't know it by what you see here, but he was a handsome, polite, intelligent man. His smile was charming and disarming at the same time. His parents granted him every whim and he rewarded them with top grades and by being an obedient son. His studies afforded him little time for mischief. He had no criminal history.

"I spoke with an aunt who, when he was about eight years old, took him into the woods after a snowfall and showed him a tree in the distance.

"'Walk toward the tree,' she said, 'and don't look at anything but the tree. Now look at your footprints.' She made him repeat the exercise until he could consistently leave a trail that was absolutely straight. She challenged him to set his sights on an object and not look anywhere but towards it until he had achieved his goal.

"During college he was recruited by the military for his linguistic ability. In his undergraduate studies he learned Spanish, Farsi, German, Hebrew and Greek. He was not proficient in all of them, mind you, but he was comfortable with them. He chose instead to attend a prestigious liberal seminary. He received a scholarship and completed his education through the doctorate level there. About that time, he wrote his first book and became a favorite on the speaking circuit. He received a Doctor of Theology degree, majoring in comparative religions. He could be persuasive without being argumentative. He wanted to be tops in the defense of his Christian beliefs, whether it be as a brilliant orator, prolific author, or both.

"He pastored a church for a time, and I spoke with some members of his congregation who were happy to talk with me. Saddened by his passing, many had stories they wanted to tell. I'm guessing here, but I think it was a good catharsis for some of them. Some compared him to the great preacher, Jonathan Edwards. His

15

voice would crescendo to a rousing peak, then suddenly drop to a whisper. One lady even recalled a sermon in which he said, 'Two mighty oaks grow in the forest. One grows in the shaded forest floor, receiving plenty of water and just enough sunshine. Its roots are strong. The other grows on the side of a hill, its roots struggling for water, its mighty symmetry gnarled and grotesque. When the logger comes to cut the oaks down, he almost jumps with glee at the sight of the gnarled and deformed oak. Because it has had to work so hard, its sturdy wood will make furniture that will last years and years.

"'Friends, don't fret when trials and troubles come your way. The strength that comes from them will serve to make you and keep you strong.'"

I paused for a moment and glanced at Ed. He sat motionless and expressionless.

*Are you with me, Ed? What are you thinking?* I wondered. I didn't know where he was then, but now I know, for I have been to 'that place' many times.

"He wrote numerous books in defense of Christianity." I went on, trying not to sound droll.

"Professors acquainted with him academically told me about a year or so back he began to research the life of the Emperor Nero for a book he was writing on First Century Christianity. His research turned to obsession. He studied the turmoil of the Jews and the times they were living; the struggle of civilization under Roman oppression. He appreciated Nero for his tolerance toward other religions, and how he managed to keep Rome at her pinnacle through twelve difficult years.

"'Paul's colleagues began to worry. As his affection for this man-who-would-be-a-god increased, Dr. Anderson's values began to change. He had studied many major religions and up until recently, kept their dogmas at an arm's length from his own Christian beliefs, but, then he began to speak privately about how he was finding Christianity more and more oppressive. He soon became outspoken against Christians who insisted theirs was the only way.

"A professor from his first college told me that Dr. Anderson had read the Bible many times and knew it inside out. The professor added that Paul knew the Master, but did not serve Him."

Again I had to pause. I knew what this professor was talking about, but I had not given religion much thought. *Was this the key?*

*Was this the reason Ed gave me this case?... to study the life of a man who knew what he believed, but not why? Was Ed trying to foist religion on me?*

"Dr. Anderson read that sometime around A.D. 68 Nero had Paul the Apostle beheaded. Historians agree that around this time Nero went utterly mad and began a barbaric persecution of the Christians. Paul Anderson sided with Nero. After all, it must have been something they did to provoke him to wrath.

"Christians insisted that they were the light of the world. That could never be, according to Nero. He was a god himself. He was light.

"Over the course of a few short months Dr. Anderson's speeches evolved into blathering diatribes. He publicly renounced any vestige of Christianity he might have been clinging to. He turned apologetics into a weapon and used it to convince others of the dangers in the teachings of organized religion. He ranted and raved, sometimes going on for hours in front of anyone who would listen. He showed up in class and in the pulpit in wrinkled suits, needing a shave. One day he did not bother to show up at all.

'They found him a few days later barricaded in his home, filthy and mumbling incoherently. The doctors locked him up, under constant watch for his safety's sake. A pattern emerged. At certain times of the night he would scream and tear at his clothes and back into a corner of his cell, eyes seeing only what he alone could see. On the night he died, he curled up in a ball and shook for hours howling, 'Nero, save me! Nero, save me!' Those were the last words he ever spoke."

I was exhausted just telling the story. I shuffled papers, not wishing to betray my feelings in front of Ed. After a moment or two of silence he spoke. "Interesting story. You certainly learned a lot more about the man than I did."

He motioned for me to follow him and we walked to his office. "Look here." He removed a book from a shelf. "This is a *Commentary on the Epistles of Paul the Apostle* written by Dr. Paul Anderson, an absolutely tremendous work."

He got up to leave. Almost as an afterthought, he looked back at me. "Do you see why I hoped you would run with this case? Do you see why the other directors here are interested in tasks that you deem mundane? You have learned a lot about your man in there. I hope there is still room for you to learn a bit about yourself."

# Chapter 4:

# You'll Be Lost and You'll Be Sorry When I'm Gone

Iprepared Dr. Anderson for the crematory, although there was not much I could do. I talked to him as I worked. I renamed him "The Howling Man." His limbs and mouth would not budge. He was defiant even in death, but was he feeling anything now?

*Hey, young man,* I could sense him speaking. *Be real sure of what you believe because you don't get a chance to change your mind later on. Don't lose sight of your first love."*

I felt a shudder. Was it possible that such a learned man could ever be wrong about anything? Was he wrong even now? Looking down upon what had once been a powerful and gifted human, I was truly sad. No one came to pay their respects, to cry over him, to grieve. I had done all I could. I could not prolong his fate further. Cremation involves subjecting the remains to a fire of about 1720 degrees, the entire process requiring about three hours. I made a silent vow to at least try to treat clients such as Paul with empathy and respect, but what to do now? I had no options but to break his legs so they would fit inside the crematory where he could meet his demons head on. I was not overly religious at the time, but I said a silent prayer that people I knew could be spared such fearful agony as this.

I'll admit I am not an astute observer, but I thought I was a quick learner. I thought I was handling myself in a manner more to Ed's liking. Apparently not. The weeks dragged on and it seemed that I was being assigned more than my fair share of routine cremations. There were a few in which I glanced superficially into their past, but it seemed the vast majority died of mediocrity.

Looking back at the beginning of my career, I remember taking no pride nor finding any sense of worth at a cremation of the poor, the indigent, the unknown and the unwanted. *That would be their fate; tending them would be mine*, I remember thinking. What made matters worse, many of these cases had to be completed after hours, so there were numerous occasions where I would leave work for the day only to be called back at night to sit by the crematory. State law required the crematory be attended by a licensed director at all times while in use.

On wintry nights it was a nice place to get comfortable with a book. Ed had allowed the installation of a television, and some people brought music, but however placid I could make this scene, this was not a Currier and Ives moment, and I certainly did not want to make a career of it.

Paul Anderson cried out to me. *You're wrong, Son! No life is mediocre. Think of us as you release us. As for yourself, don't gamble. Eternity is not a bet you can afford to lose.*

*What had he meant by that? Would I ever see him again?* The Howling Man had been a diversion, long past.

Then one day, Ed called me into the office to inform me that I was to be the recipient of a case in which the decedent had asked for a casket burial, church funeral and graveside services. The man had arranged a 'pre-need' and had asked for the top-of-the-line casket, and hundreds of dollars in florals. It certainly looked like he was entitled. His family was one of the wealthiest in the city. I was stunned and pleased. Usually these types of cases were reserved for the boss himself. He was entrusting the good name and reputation of his establishment to me. Finally! My time was at hand! So why did I notice a niggling doubt creeping into my thoughts?

The following day, Mr. John Alford II arrived. He was naked, stripped of all the vestiges that people wore when they wanted to exude power and wealth. It was difficult to imagine him as he once was, literally a captain of industry. He was placed in the cooler to await the family's wishes.

19

Perhaps that little niggling, or perhaps something else, compelled me, but I found myself returning to stare at his face several times that day. His lips, in death, froze into what appeared to be a smile. Now, there were certainly people that died in peace and they seemed to carry a resigned, contended look with them into eternity. But the more I looked at Mr. Alford, the more it seemed that he was wearing a grin. Malevolent? Something akin to the Cheshire Cat? "And I know something you don't" grin? Or perhaps just a peaceful, contented grin? Maybe the family could help me figure it out.

Later that day, the three Alford sons arrived and were ushered into the conference room. I offered them coffee or tea, but they declined. All three of these men dressed in the finest that money could buy – Armani suits, Magnanni shoes and handmade silk ties by Runyon. Their hairstyles were different, but each was coiffed to perfection. They treated me deferentially, their demeanor lightly tinged with haughtiness and disdain. Mostly, they were in a hurry and wanted the whole procedure done quickly and as unobtrusively as possible. They really did not want to be involved. They certainly did not look like a family in grief.

I welcomed such affluence and high society in a place such as Carson's and tried to force small talk. Bad move.

"You and your father must have traveled all over the world."

They looked at each other. One son finally nodded and with effort said, "Yes, we did"

I groped for an opening. "I imagine you have met some very famous people."

The same son spoke again, condescension evident. "Yes, but no one with a name recognizable from tabloid headlines."

They stood up. I took that as a cue, and ended all pretense of attempting light conversation. Time to complete the business transaction. They presented the establishment with three separate personal checks totaling nineteen thousand dollars. I could barely conceal my delight. Now it was my turn to usher them out as soon as I could do so without being obvious. Would Ed be pleased, or what? One of the sons handed me a large box that contained the funeral clothes. I resisted the urge to look inside at the time, but my guess was they would be as expensively tailored, if not more so, than the suits they were wearing.

The funeral was to take place within 72 hours at St. Mark's Episcopal Church. The sons were assured that Carson's would handle all the details in strict accordance with their wishes. They left, and I felt better at the parting. Something was terribly strange, but I had a lot of work to do on this one.

I presented the checks to Ed with a flourish, but they seemingly made no impact. He tucked them carelessly in a desk drawer much as if he was filing an old business card. He leaned back in his chair and said, "If you care to listen to some advice, be careful you don't become like this family. With so much money involved, their business is their religion. Their offices are their temples. If you are ever interested, after the funeral I would be delighted to tell you the story. Good luck with your case."

Wordlessly, I left the office, in a hurry to begin work. I put Ed's admonition in the back of my mind, but, unlike the warning he gave me as I dealt with Mr. Thomas, I did not immediately dismiss it. In fact, the more I looked at the man the more uneasy I became, and I couldn't explain it. I removed Mr. Alford from the cooler and applied a powerful astringent to his face that would smooth out the majority of the wrinkles. He was eighty-one years old, and I was determined to make him appear mature and patriarchal – stern-faced and commanding respect... a man obviously from high society and wealth. His facial expression needed very little work. The more I stared, the more difficult it was to tell if his lips were forming a grin or a sneer, but I couldn't change them without changing his entire demeanor. After completing this initial phase, I placed him back in his assigned spot in the cooler. There would be no need to work on him until the following day. The next order of business was to call the secretary at St. Mark's. She assured us that all preparations were underway, and it could hold the large number of people that were expected.

Carson's held no binding contracts with any one florist. Ed preferred to help fledgling, deserving businesses, so he generally used a privately-owned florist that in Ed's eyes, had proven reliable, providing quality work, and was not part of a big chain corporation. Mr. Alford's sons left strict instructions that this was to be a huge and ostentatious affair with fresh flowers, grandly arrayed at the church and the cemetery, sculpted into unique designs as the florist saw fit. The florist assured me they would rise to the occasion. The suit was removed from its box and arranged on hangars, to be pressed later, if necessary. As I suspected, it was indeed, a suit fit for this "king."

I left work that night recreating the scenario in my mind. *Had anything been left to chance?*

Looking back, I remember the Alford case especially because it was a rare time in which I contemplated and wrestled with questions that had no answers. *Why was so much money being spent on a corpse? As a culture, we tend to place little value on the living, so why are the dead worth so much more? Has there ever been enough money spent on a funeral to pay off feelings of guilt? I did not own much of a suit, but I was working on a dead man arrayed like King Solomon himself. Hundreds spent in flowers? He's just as dead.*

I remember not being able to fall asleep because I was wrestling with Ed's statement and I was curious about the part of a story yet to be learned... "Don't be like this family."

*Don't be like the sons? The father? Why had I been assigned this case? What did Ed think he knew about me that I did not know about myself?*

The next day was one day away from the Main Event. I took Mr. Alford out of the cooler and removed the excess astringent cream applied the day before. The result was what I had hoped for. The skin cells had shriveled, much of the water exiting them in the process. This resulted in tighter looking cheeks and forehead, and removal of a number of wrinkles. It took twenty years off his face. Then it was back to the cooler to let the skin air-dry. A few hours later, I returned to apply just the right amount of skin toner and a touch of pale pink to the lips. He would be presented to the mourners as he had been known. I had learned that lesson well!

Next would be a break from applying makeup in order to dress him. Shirt, tie, pants, socks and shoes, even though the linens in the casket covered his legs. It is not easy putting pants and shirt on a corpse, and it took two people to do so. Some establishments are known for slitting the shirt and jacket down the back so they would not need to struggle with limp arms and legs, but the majority, including Carson's, would not hear of this.

Ed was in and out as usual, smiling, looking over my shoulder but saying nothing. Finally, I cornered one of the retrieval technicians and we settled Mr. Alford into one of the most beautiful caskets he had ever seen. Call it a casket, call it what you will. This was a finely crafted work of art. A beautiful African hardwood with a silver patterned inlay. Lifting the lid open, I shuddered to think of the job that awaited the pallbearers. Mr. Alford weighed around 180 pounds, and the casket would double the load.

Once we had him nestled inside, I arranged his hands as he requested; open and beckoning. Mr. Alford had specifically asked for this gesture. As I was to learn later, Mr. Alford loved his sons and wanted to embrace them. I admitted to Ed that its meaning would most likely be lost on them. A white carnation in his lapel and a very expensive silk kerchief in his breast pocket completed the preparations. He was about ready. Then it was back to the cooler for the night to await a final inspection before the viewing at the church.

I stepped back and admired my work. It was complete.

The following day I arrived at the office, excited and anticipating the day's events. I removed Mr. Alford one last time, touched up his makeup and smoothed his clothes. Another director and I would officiate, but I was the lead. We loaded the casket into the back of the gray/black hearse with the aid of a hydraulic cart. Once at the church we would ask for volunteers to help us carry it to the front for the viewing.

We arrived one hour early to find that the florists had been true to their word and then some. The flowers and their settings were idyllic and arranged perfectly. Brilliant orange lilies, some late spring blooming potted plants, white and yellow carnations, all resting on a field of green, the entire color splash contrasting perfectly against the backdrop of the ivory walls of the church. It was a stunning display costing hundreds on the one hand, but a short-lived brilliance destined for some local nursing home after the service. The church itself, and now the flowers, were a testimony to the awesome talent in man's hands. It was all quite regal and breathtaking.

I sighed as I surveyed the magnificent church, the stone-faced people and Mr. Alford. It was a rather peculiar setting in which to eulogize a man; here in this place before an altar to an unknown God that I, and most of the mourners present did not know or care to know.

People began filtering in. Fifteen minutes prior to the start of the service, we were surprised that there were so few in attendance. Of the men there, almost all wore the requisite dark suit, subtle tie, and pained expression. I caught snippets of conversation, and it seemed like everyone wanted to be somewhere else.

"Hey. Vanessa and I would like you to come for dinner sometime…"

"Jeff down in accounts picked up his new car. He was showing it off… we all oohed and aahed over it. Not my cup of tea."

"Look at the suit Dan is wearing. If he wants to suck up to the boss, he ought to have better taste in clothes."

The sons arrived and took their places in front, glancing furtively about during the entire service. They would soon inherit all their father's earthly goods. It appeared that they wanted out of here as fast as possible to begin their new life of wealth, social climbing, and any other rewards they thought they deserved. In fact, when it came time for personal eulogies, they were hard pressed for words. They had plenty of notice that they would be speaking. They readily volunteered to be featured, yet all they could do was to stumble and mutter meaningless platitudes.

*Was it grief or had they given absolutely no thought to what they should say about a man who had been their father for over forty years? Was it just plain boredom? These boys assumed they were about to inherit millions, yet they could show no more animation than this?*

"Uh…he was a good man and a kind man and I will miss him."

"Well, umm, if he can hear me, I would like to thank him for being my father."

"I can't add much more to what my brothers said, and I most certainly agree."

The only person showing genuine emotion and crying genuine tears was Ms. Alford, and in the world of Mr. Alford's sons, neither they nor any person in that church stepped forward to comfort her, no one cared enough to even place an arm around her.

Halfway through the service, I glanced around from my vantage point at the rear of the church. People had arrived fashionably late, but there was still plenty of open seating available. Finally, it was our turn. We opened the lid of the casket and stood by as people filed past. Most had a bland look about them and shuffled by with barely a glance. To cap off one of the strangest services I had ever witnessed, the sons were to be three of the pall bearers and were supposed to have chosen three more. Of course, they had not and now had difficulty finding anyone. They scrambled about until they corralled the last three men remaining in the church.

We closed the casket over a still-grinning John Alford II, locked it, and accompanied the unwilling pall bearers as they hefted it back to and inside the hearse. A short procession found its way to the cemetery.

Again, the flower array was magnificent, especially in the bright sun with the blue sky as a backdrop. No more than twenty people

listened as the pastor consigned Mr. Alford to his Maker with what
sounded like a stern admonition to the sons.

"What does it profit a man to gain the whole world and lose his
soul? What price can one pay to redeem his own soul? The heart of
this man that is all too soon swallowed up by the good earth lies still
and empty. Were all the good deeds he did in his life enough to allow
him entrance into Heaven? I think not! Will all his wealth earn him a
seat at the King's table? Of course not! To those who can hear, beware!
Knowing God in this life is not a religion, it is a relationship!"

Now he addressed his words to the deceased. "John Alford,
we here at your church love you as you loved us. You gave out of
genuine warmth, not just because you could. We know that at this
moment you are standing in front of Jesus Christ, The Almighty, and
are listening as He says, 'Well done, thou good and faithful servant…
enter into the joy of your Lord.' And for those of us that remain and
mourn your passing, all I can hope is that we can look at ourselves
and say, it is well, truly well, with our souls."

*Nice sermon, I thought, but it is not for me, not now anyway.
Besides, I'm still young. I've got plenty of time to worry about
choosing a god. But I remember the uneasy feeling too. Was it well
with my soul?*

I looked at the sons. They were looking at their watches,
polishing their fingernails; seemingly bored with it all.

Then it was over. Attendants and pallbearers secured straps
about the casket and lowered it into the grave. The attendees threw
their boutonnières after it. A sexton maneuvering a backhoe came and
unceremoniously covered the man. The crowd dispersed. Very neat,
cut, dried and finished.

At home after work that night, I reviewed the day's events.
Much as had been the experience with Mr. Thomas, the planning had
been flawless. The preparations done to a "T." The result was terribly
anticlimactic. Yet I wondered. *How was this supposed to affect me, if at
all? Were there still character flaws in me I could not see?*

I reviewed the overt behavior of the sons and the smattering of
mourners that could be bothered to show up that day. They seemed
cold, aloof, interested in their own comforts, and narrow-minded. The
whole service was different from most. There were few tears. No one
stood to eulogize an obviously great man; no one interacted with Mrs.
Alford. *What sort of a family was this?* My thoughts, as I drifted off

into an uneasy sleep, were *Does Ed see me in the sons? I certainly don't see myself that way.*

Days passed. I was in the office catching up on routine paperwork when Ed motioned for me to come to the office. He was not alone. "There is someone here I would like you to meet."

We headed for the office. Ed assumed his usual posture, leaning back in his rickety desk chair with his hands interlocked behind his head. He smiled. "I assume you are anxious to hear the whole story about Mr. Alford," he began.

"Yes, I am sort of curious about that," I admitted.

He leaned forward suddenly as if about to relate a sacred mystery, then he began. "Some time back I met with Mr. Alford and his lawyer." He motioned to the man sitting in the other chair. "They swore me to secrecy and insisted I do everything his way if I wanted his business. I agreed, insisting they convince me there would be nothing illegal or immoral. They assured me all was above-board.

"Mr. Alford had three sons. He was away from home for extended periods of time, often on business, but he tried to be a good father nonetheless. His wife died when the youngest was five. He remarried. His new wife tried to love the boys, but by then it was too late, the damage done. They saw in their parents a means to an end. All too early, they became aware of the sense of entitlement afforded to the very wealthy, and they began to have little use for anyone, including their parents. Nannies came and went. The boys traveled with their father, not only because he wanted them with him, but because he was eager to teach them the family business and, of course, show them that people who handle millions of dollars can be handled with honesty and morality."

"I met them. A difficult encounter, to say the least."

Ed nodded and continued. "Soon the father realized that all three boys had the same desires: inherit the family fortune and cruise through life. They felt they were entitled. The father became bitter. He had worked hard and dealt honestly with people in his business dealings. He wanted his name remembered in that way. Unknown to the boys, he began giving his money to charity. He worked less diligently, let accounts lapse, and amassed debt. His debtors didn't mind; they knew his name was worth their time. The Alford Hotel downtown, as a matter of fact, is still solvent, and its furnishings could be sold to cover his loans. We will see how that plays into his scheme in a bit.

"Soon, his friends and partners began to worry. His name moved mountains in the financial world, so his credit would always be honored, but he was looking bad on paper. Most of his endeavors were no longer turning a profit."

"I think I know what happened next..."

Ed went on and dismissed me with a wave of his hand. "When he and his lawyer first met with me, they let me know that his will stipulated that all his holdings, properties, cash, etc. was to be divided equally among his three sons. He sat down with each of them and told them of the will. He also informed them that they could each accept cash from him in the amount of one million dollars each while he was alive, and give up their part of the will. All opted to wait, assuming there was much more to be had. What was more discouraging to him was that they were almost gleeful in their anticipation. All this talk of wills certainly meant that death was imminent, didn't it? His last proviso was that they hold a lavish funeral for him, the bigger the better. He told them because the funeral home wanted cash up front that they would need to pay for this out of their own pockets. He did set aside a trust to pay his wife a small monthly stipend for the remainder of her life, or until she remarries. He also gave her $250,000 cash up front."

"That's all she gets out of this?"

"Now wait a minute, we have a ways to go. The sons eagerly accepted all of their father's stipulations. They were aware that the lawyer would be present, making sure all was according to Mr. Alford's wishes. This is Mr. Schleisser, the lawyer, and I imagine he is here to tell us the rest of the story."

Without much of a smile, Mr. Schleisser snapped open his briefcase, removed some papers and began speaking. His thick accent, German I assumed, made it difficult to understand and I leaned forward in my seat. "Mr. Alford, through the years, retained a battery of lawyers. He consulted with me a while ago. You see, he knew he was dying. He had some sort of brain disease that would take his life, but unfortunately it would take its toll on his mental faculties before killing him. He knew he was slipping, and wanted to make solid arrangements before he lost his ability to think clearly. In a nutshell, all the conditions of the will were met. The sons have inherited all of the late Mr. Alford's properties. At his death, Mr. Alford owed tens-of-millions, payable on demand, and all notes are past due. As we speak, banks are writing liens and foreclosures on his houses and businesses. His jet is for sale, as well as his modest collection of artwork and antiques. He had various dealings with the city, and the building that is The Alford Hotel is to be given to the City of Portland, Oregon, but its contents is the sole property of Mrs. Alford. I am sad to say that the only thing the boys inherited was a huge debt that, even should all these sales be a success, will still be quite substantial. Any further assets they may acquire will go to pay the debts of the estate.

"So you see, my young friend, the wife truly loved him unconditionally, and was well cared for. Mr. Alford gave stern instructions that she was not to provide the boys with anything other than modest gifts for special occasions, and as the executor of the estate, I will see that his conditions are upheld. Good day."

With that, he stood up, made a small bow at the waist, and showed himself out.

Ed continued. "In addition, Mr. Alford wrote that the boys would each need to be present in either the house or a business every day for one week. Before you came in, Mr. Schleisser said that they watched as trucks pulled up, day after day, truck after truck, and workers stripped walls bare, wheeled out furniture, etc. It was all quite depressing." Ed was not smiling.

"Take stock of yourself. Your clients may be dead, but learn from them. You're young; that's not your fault. Look closely at the cases I'm assigning you. I'm treating you like I have all the people that started out working here. I want you to take away lessons from those that failed and from those that had a measure of success. Trust me on this. If you work strictly for personal gain, your reward will come quickly and vanish just as quickly. But if you stay with us you will be enriched. I will give you some cases that will provoke you to deep thought. If you choose, your research will provide you with insight into human character and therefore, contentment. If you work strictly for a check, you will be miserable all your life, wherever it is you decide to settle."

*Mr. Alford, his sons, myself. Would I be willing to be set into a casket with my arms stretched, beckoning in love to my children? Would that gesture be lost on them?*

I could almost hear Mr. Alford's voice years later. "My boys made a wreck of their lives early on, but they were still my boys. I miss them."

The preacher's words rang in my ears. It was truly not well with my soul. *How did Ed know? Was my deportment that obvious?* I opened my mouth to explain, to defend myself, but nothing came out.

"Wherever you go, at least for now, you have the luxury of time. We were all like you, but we learned what is important, what is not. I don't care if you go, but I hope you stay. Just do yourself a favor and don't leave until you are able to take some valuable lessons with you. Oh... and in case you're interested, every director here with the exception of yourself has been here over 25 years." He added with a snicker, "Guess we're still learning, eh?"

With that he turned his back to me and took up papers on his desk. It was a polite dismissal, and surprisingly, I wasn't offended.

Alone, at night in my study, I sensed the lesson that Mr. Alford was trying to get across to me. *I was grieving because I was watching my boys...,* he was saying, *...the looks on their faces as all they held dear was stripped away. I worry about their future. I look at my country which has the finest government that mankind could create, and I see that making strong laws and a strong economy are admirable, but there will never be enough money printed to satisfy greed. So I cried for my sons, and, my friend, if you had just taken the time to look at my face you would have noticed the tears.*

# Chapter 5:

# We Sing So She Can Slumber

So it was. It took years, but I was learning. Learning how to be at peace with myself and to understand that the living and the dead would be delighted to guide me through life, if I would just become a willing participant. It was and is a lengthy work in progress.

Many of the more notable cases assigned to me are consigned to memory, or at least in my files. Occasionally, I re-visit the dead, and I remember those that helped get me where I am today.

Case in point: Mrs. Beatrice Jessel.

It was almost 4:00 p.m. and work was winding down for the day. I was preparing a tiny, elderly lady for viewing by her husband prior to cremation. She was almost 90, non-descript in a sea of other elderly women that had come and gone. I had no specific instructions on how to set her, but I worked to do my best. Unfortunately, the only material I had to go by was a black and white photo the husband gave Ed, which was, I assumed, a wedding picture. Ed had told me that this couple had been married 70 years. The husband had worked in a mine and on a particular day, a group of young men had asked for the day off so they could go into town and get married.

Seriously?

Never having met his bride-to-be, this man married on one day, and stayed on with the same woman for 70 years.

I was almost finished with the preparations, awaiting the husband who would arrive shortly.

As expected, Ed came into the viewing area accompanied by a small, elderly man who had a hat in his hands, furiously working the brim. His eyes darted about and took in the room, not yet focusing on his wife. His cheeks were tear-stained. I introduced myself and told Mr. Jessel I would be outside, and to take his time. Ed and I left.

As we were walking toward the office, we noticed several cars pulling into the parking lot. As they disgorged their passengers, we noticed that there were at least a dozen people, predominately female, all dressed in various sorts of hospital garb. We stood and watched as one approached us and asked for instructions on where they could see Mrs. Jessel. Ed pointed to the viewing room and told them Mr. Jessel was already visiting. The young lady thanked us and left to relay this information to the others. They all walked across the parking lot and disappeared behind the door.

We shrugged our shoulders and headed to the office to await their departure. I would then return Mrs. Jessel to the cooler and cremate her first thing in the morning.

Cremation could not take place until we had the signed death certificate, and the Medical Examiner had assured me it would arrive early the following day.

About twenty minutes went by and the group began trickling out. Almost all were in tears. I left the office quickly, my curiosity piqued. I tapped one of the ladies on the shoulder and asked her if she would be willing to come into the office for coffee or a soft drink and tell us what had just transpired. She agreed.

The three of us settled into our chairs and she began. "My name is Mindy and I am a registered nurse. Most of the people you saw are nurses, or they work on our floor in the hospital.

"We met Mrs. Jessel about two months ago. She was admitted with the problems that most people of her age experience at the end of life – heart failure, bad kidneys – but the worst thing for her, and us, was she was absolutely out of her mind, demented. To top it off, she was a screamer and she swung at the staff. We knew she could not help it, but it made it nearly impossible to care for her. She had a cruel streak; and believe me, after you have been a nurse for as long as I have, you know a cruel streak when you see it. Frankly, I think the nursing home was using any excuse to have her admitted so she would be off their hands.

"We grew to really despise having to deal with her. She was a liability, a chore, a burden, anything else you could think. She was a chronically ill patient who was not going to get better no matter how much modern medicine could offer; just the type of person that most of the staff do not like to care for. She would be with us until she died, which could have been days or months. I mean, what could we save her from? Our loathing became more virulent, almost palpable. It was made even more difficult because we had no outlet for our bitterness.

"She was a mess; we were a mess. She soiled her sheets and then threw her linens at us. Other patients complained about the horrific noise. Visitors complained about the smell. Soon, only the male nurses cared for her because they were just better at avoiding her flailing arms.

"It was funny, you know? The only respite we had from the noise was when her husband came. He would come in upbeat and then we would tell him of her day, and we tried to be nice, but the best we could do was just avoid him. But he knew. He could see it in our eyes, our body language."

She paused. "By the time he walked into her room, we had successfully robbed him of his smile, and his shoulders stooped from the weight of feelings we couldn't hide. He would almost always leave in tears, but for the time he was inside, there was peace. Blessed peace."

She paused again, and shook her head slowly from side to side. "God, we were so bitter," she mumbled almost to herself.

She took a deep sigh and continued. "One day we finally figured out we should try to see what he was doing to keep her quiet. Each time we tried to break our busy routines and watch him; it seemed to never work out. We were always interrupted. Finally one of the nurses asked him what he did when he was with her by himself.

He told us that for the last thirty years of his marriage, every night, without fail, just before they fell asleep, he would sing to her... the same song. Every night for thirty years he sang:

> *Let me call you sweetheart, I'm in love with you*
> *Let me hear you whisper that you love me too*
> *Keep the love-light glowing in your eyes so blue*
> *Let me call you sweetheart, I'm in love with you."*
> (*Let Me Call You Sweetheart;* music by Leo Friedman,
> lyrics by Beth Whitson, 1910)

Ed nodded, his somber look replaced by his usual grin, along with a somewhat knowing look. I had never heard the song.

She finished her story. "So what was there to do? After the story got around, we tried to figure out what to do with the information. Turns out we didn't have long to wait. Beatrice died a few days later. We watched as they carried her away. The husband had that shuffle that signified that he was horribly defeated, had lost everything. He was devastated; destroyed. How much of that had been our fault was anybody's guess. We sat around trying to figure out some way to right this wrong, and what we had to do suddenly hit us. We got together and came up with what we hoped would be a beautiful conclusion to this couple's life. We joined Mr. Jessel in your room there a few minutes ago, and we sang Mrs. Jessel into eternity with a chorus of, 'Let Me Call You Sweetheart.'

Some of us nurses, hardened by years on the front lines, may have grown a bit softer."

*Hey, Beatrice,* I thought, *if there is a ladies club up there, filled with those who have been married to the same man over 50 years; if you see a beautiful black haired lady up there who answers to the name "Adelina," tell her that her husband is heartbroken. He wants to sing her a song but he can't remember the words.*

She got up to leave and we both accompanied her to her car. We saw Mr. Jessel a few moments later. His shuffling was different. His eyes were just a bit brighter, his head held a little bit higher. Grief and sorrow were there, but they walked alongside of him, instead of weighing him down. He had 70 years of unconditional love from Mrs. Jessel to carry him through the remainder of his life and in addition, perhaps the silent admiration of some hospital employees who might now be able to bear their own burdens a bit easier.

If the souls of the people who came that day to sing the tribute were changed, I'll never know. Just perhaps, there were some young, overconfident, brash nurses and one stubborn funeral director who would, for the first time, realize the paycheck is not the only thing that could 'prick the conscience of the king.'

# Chapter 6:
# The Night of the Meek

I was only a few years into the profession, working on treating the individual with compassion. But change does not come overnight and there were outbursts of the old Me. I had yet to fully tame my ego and selfish nature. Perhaps a young boy named Billy Jameson could help.

There was a stir in the building as people interrupted their work and made excuses to wander into Ed's office. Donna tried unsuccessfully to shoo everyone out, but to no avail. I asked Enrique, one of the retrieval techs who picked up the deceased at their place of death, what all the fuss was about.

"Willard Jameson is here to see Mr. Carson!"

"Who's Willard Jameson?"

"Man! You live in a cave? He was a nobody. Just a former great football player with the Chicago Bears who played in two Super Bowls. Everyone called him Will."

"I wonder what he could want with Carson's."

Enrique gave me an odd look. "Gee, Pal. Do you think someone may have *died*?"

Football had never been too interesting to me, but one of the other directors, craning his neck to steal a look, informed me that Jameson played under the great George Halas, perhaps the finest coach in the history of football. Now *that* name I knew.

Mr. Jameson left the office, and by the glum expression on his face, he was not about to stop and give autographs. Later that day Ed came by the preparation room and spoke with a few of the staff. "Mr. Jameson's son, Billy was found dead in his room today and he wants us to handle the arrangements. The family wants him cremated."

He motioned to me. "It's your turn." The smile returned, along with that knowing look in his eye.

Some of the staff seemed relieved. Others were disappointed. I spoke out. "Wouldn't it be better if someone who actually likes football and wants this case took it? I wouldn't mind."

Ed looked at his feet a moment and said, "Mmm..., no. It's yours. But make sure you fill us in on the great man, if tact permits."

"Okay" I said under my breath as I let out a deep sigh. "I guess the only thing to do is to make the best of it."

Billy, the death certificate, and the family all arrived about the same time the following morning. Mr. and Mrs. Jameson were ushered into the conference room while I arranged Billy on a rolling cart to begin my work. He was dressed in a plaid shirt and jeans. His thick glasses were still in place. He died at the ripe old age of forty-one. This was somewhat noteworthy because Billy was a Mongoloid child, or more appropriately, a boy born with Down Syndrome. Forty-one was a long life for people with his condition. He was one of the few people I could remember, other than Mr. Alford, who died with an air of peacefulness on his face.

When I met Willard and Betty Jameson, I had trouble reining in the "old self," who made snap judgments of people and their character and was usually wrong. All three of the people in front of me, including the deceased, looked alike. Mrs. Jameson reminded me of the darling, chubby, silver- haired grandmothers whose painted portraits graced cookie tins every Christmas. Dad looked like a very pleasant bulldog, a very heavy man with a round face. He too, wore jeans and a plaid shirt. He once had been a massive, agile defensive lineman, but there was no agility left here. Playing among other players that would be elected to the football hall of fame, Willard went mostly unnoticed. He did well and received modest accolades. At six feet, 225 pounds in his prime, he was far from being the largest defensive player on the team.

I remember thinking to myself. *What can these people teach me? After all, I hold a college degree, they do not. I have accomplishments in which I take great pride. They had a special needs child. I was young and intelligent. The Jamesons can't move in my circles.*

Sadly for me, I realized that although the latter was true, I found out that they had not the least bit of desire to do so.

I tried to look attentive and patient, but I was getting bored with the whole thing. They wanted a cremation for Billy.

*Fine. Let's get on with it.* I was in a hurry to get home. It was difficult enough working in front of an audience; their stares were slowing me down.

Occasionally Mrs. Jameson would reach a tentative hand out and adjust Billy's glasses. She told me she wanted to make sure his glasses stayed on, "because he couldn't see a thing without them."

Then Dad began to speak, with Mom chiming in occasionally. I was putting some finishing touches on the face and smoothing the hair as best I could. While I was working, and as Willard was speaking words I was not hearing somewhere in the background, I spent a few moments mentally polishing up the pedestal I had erected for myself. After Mr. Jameson lumbered up to the table to survey my handy work, he looked at me, placed a hand on my shoulder and shook my hand. He tried to mutter some words but I interrupted him with a shrug and an empty "Thank you." I was irritated and tried to do my best to sound patronizing and condescending. Mr. Jameson finally seemed to compose himself and related Billy's story while I attempted to stay aloof, caught up in my "work."

It didn't take long for Billy, a dead child with Down Syndrome, to knock me clean off the pedestal I had worked so hard to construct. A few moments into the story of this young boy and I wasn't in too much of a hurry to get home after all.

"…You see, I retired from football and married Betty, here. She could overlook an awkward man in a huge frame." Mr. Jameson said.

Betty interrupted. She was clutching her husband's arm and smiling at him approvingly. Then she looked not at me, but right through me and said, "Young man, you would do well to offer kindness and quiet courage to a mate."

Willard patted her on the arm and continued. "Betty bore me three fine children. I remember her first pregnancy. It was so exciting. It would be a boy and he would be a pro football player and then be President of the United States. But that was not to be, because the first was a girl. But no matter, I was so proud I could've burst. The second child was a boy and I was ecstatic. This was it! He would learn to throw a football before he could walk. But this was not to be either. On the second day of his life we realized that there was something wrong. The doctors confirmed it. Billy had Down Syndrome, and he would never be a big league ball player or important politician. We had a third son, perfectly normal. He is a wonderful, big, strapping boy. All of us agreed that we would treat Billy as a normal child and all would care for him.

"My Billy loved to play, and he loved playing with Daddy. Speech was difficult but he 'invented' a game and named it using the only phonetics he could master at the time. 'Pookie- Pookie' was his version of standing up and tickling someone while being tickled himself. It would end up with both parties going to their knees, and finally on their bellies, wrestling and tickling each other."

Willard paused and it was clear that he was reliving a powerful moment. Betty stood quietly, eyes moist.

"The Good Lord has allowed me to maintain a small amount of name recognition from football days. I run my own business and have a little time to do some motivational speaking. We could always give our children everything they needed, and what Billy needed most of all was time. He would wait at home, poised on his knees on the couch, staring out the window waiting for the car to pull into the driveway. Then he would jump off and race about yelling *'Daaa Daa!'* No matter what I was dressed in, and it was usually a suit and tie, he would tug at me, ready to play Pookie-Pookie."

Betty chuckled. "So here was this huge man in a suit rolling around on the floor with a giggling boy who was a pretty big kid himself. Our other children would bring their friends home wanting an introduction to Willard and wanting to look at some of his trophies, but he just would not get up and shake their hands. He was too busy rolling around on the floor."

Willard shook his head sadly. "I love all my children, and they love me, but I have never seen as much unconditional love as Billy returned. Pure and dependent... a heck of a lot more than his 'normal' siblings ever showed.

"We are a church-going family. We tried to teach Billy what he could grasp about God and Heaven, but did any of it stick? I don't know. He and my other son, Derrick, shared a room and Derrick would tell me that Billy would lie on his back in the dark and say 'Psst! Psst! God? Are You there?'

"Billy grew to be a big boy, just like me. His cognitive ability never progressed much past the Pookie Pookie stage, and he had about enough dexterity to feed himself. He had no worries about food, clothes or shelter. He achieved what we all wish we could, a contentment with what he had. In time, he had his troubles. He began to have pains and slow down. As is common with Down babies, there were underlying health problems. He became severely short of breath. The doctors found a heart murmur, most likely from some defect present at birth. There was nothing to be done about it. Billy didn't mind the trips to the doctor. It was just another adventure. He remained all smiles. A few weeks later, I was tucking him into bed and he looked at me with that big old grin of his and said 'Daaa Daa, I am going to play Pookie Pookie with God.' The next morning we found him dead and at peace."

By now, the tears were rolling down both their faces, and I had to admit I wasn't feeling so cheery myself.

They did not wish to stay behind and witness the cremation. Many relatives cringe at the thought of watching their loved ones being rolled into the dark, foreboding maw that is seen when the crematory door is open. They would return the following day to claim the remains. I let them linger. They stared at their son and cried.

After a while they composed themselves and Mr. Jameson spoke again. "Billy was called to go up. We will see him soon enough, perhaps in a warrior's garb, perhaps in a shepherd's robe. He overcame and confounded the scholars and philosophers in his simplicity. They may laugh and scoff, but the sound that is the faith of one little man will be glorious. In Heaven, if the saints listen very carefully, it might even sound like Pookie Pookie."

They left, not soon enough for me. For the first time in a long time, I was uncomfortable with myself and I was glad no one would be a witness to it.

I put Billy in the crematory and stood, lost in a trance, thinking about him and his family. How long I stood there was anybody's guess, but I felt Ed tapping me on the shoulder. Jolted back into the present, we walked back to the viewing room.

Ed leaned against the door and said, "I know a little about this family. Mr. Jameson had been to some other places before he chose us. I, in turn, took a chance on choosing you. How did I do?"

It was my turn to grin. "You know," I said, "if I stay here long enough, I just might learn something."

Ed smiled and then turned wistful. "Many years ago when I started, I was just like you. Technically, there was no one better. Doing that part of the job well was satisfying for perhaps a year. Back then, waking up dreading coming to work replaced simple job satisfaction. I immersed myself in education, earning two Bachelor's degrees... business and chemistry. That did nothing to change my boredom. Finally, I became friends with a local pastor who advised me to get to know my clients and tailor to their needs, even in death. It made all the difference."

He walked out and I consigned Billy to the flames.

Before I had my own kids I used to think about Billy Jameson. I used to feel sorry for him. One night in my thoughts, I imagined I heard him laughing good-naturedly at me.

*"Hey Michael!"* he was saying. *"When I was there I had everything I wanted. All my needs were met, and I was the recipient of unconditional love. You are unsure of yourself, worried about the amount of the next paycheck, and have no faith; no hope. I had no desire for Heaven, and you feel sorry for me?"*

When most people get to Heaven, they will be surprised by the thrones, the grandeur, the peace, the streets of gold, the mansions, eternal security and the harmony between all. But you know? I don't think Billy will be surprised at all.

# Chapter 7:
# The Odyssey of Misha Kloski

Flipping through my loose diary of cases, I began to see where the evolution began in the way I saw people and myself. The dead friends I was meeting were helping me through rough times of soul-searching when I was at an impasse. For a time, I struggled almost daily to get out of bed. I just couldn't face more emptier, meaningless or lonely days.

I had always assumed I would get through life and my job just by going through the motions. Get up, go to work, get paid, pay the bills, but my dead friends and Ed, my boss, were convincing me that no one can survive "intact" by just doing that. I had to get involved, but how?

Ed, long since deceased, called himself a Christian, but he had a passage etched on a placard hanging on a wall in his office that puzzled me for the longest time. Not in its meaning per se, but in its seeming contradiction in what Christianity taught. The quote was a familiar one:

> *...Each man's death diminishes me*
> *For I am involved in mankind*
> *Therefore, send not to know for whom the bell tolls*
> *It tolls for thee."*
> (*No Man is an Island* by John Donne)

*Hey, Ed. I know you can see this, but at your passing I took that plaque home and it is still hanging in my study. I learned, Ed... really I did. I can't wait to tell you all about it.*

*Once the people came to our establishment, wasn't it too late for them? Once a person caught a glimpse of Hell, was it too late to change their mind? Was that what the Howling Man was trying to tell me? Is he still in torment?*

Much later in my career, several of my clients "explained" it to me, and I understood. They taught me many other valuable lessons as well. They scolded me about my character, and I came away dejected after taking stock of myself. My strength of character was woefully inadequate.

If I ever do make it to Heaven, Misha Kloski was a man I have put on my list of people to meet so I can shake his hand and thank him personally for keeping me on the path that Billy Jameson started me on. Even now, if I ever begin feeling a bit too confident in my own abilities, a bit too comfortable with a character that goads me into thinking I can do it all on my own, I remember...

It started as another non-descript day years ago. Enrique yanked open the heavy back doors of the van and the cart clattered as its frame opened automatically and the wheels settled to the cement. He wheeled it inside, and we unzipped the shroud.

The deceased was a tall man, in his mid-eighties. He was naked except for a long- sleeve shirt of some sort, resembling long underwear. It was quite soiled and the neck of the shirt was open several inches down, appearing to have been cut with scissors.

As I was contemplating his strange attire, a small station wagon pulled up abruptly in front of the garage. Death is usually no laughing matter, but it was difficult to keep a straight face as all four doors opened and six rather large and lanky people extricated themselves. It reminded me of a circus event.

A man approached me, hat in hand. Apparently he was the spokesman, because he spoke in very broken English. "Please, Sir. Misha. You no burn. Please? No burn!" He was pleading and frantic at the same time.

I told him that was not my decision to make, and I pointed to the office where they would need to make arrangements. Meanwhile, I introduced myself to the deceased, whose nametag read Misha. He was a well-built man, strong, probably Polish, I thought. All his papers seemed to be in order, and I fitted him with another identifying band around his ankle, then tucked him in the cooler to await further developments.

I didn't have long to wait. I noticed the troupe exiting the office. Two women were crying, and the men were gesturing wildly. They walked my way in a manner I hoped was not menacing. The spokesman repeated, "You no burn." They somehow melted back inside the small wagon and roared off.

Ed stood outside the office, shading his eyes from the unseasonably bright sun, watching. He ambled over to the garage and filled me in with a chuckle. "Poor Donna will never be the same. The crowd has successfully shaken her quite a bit. I don't believe I have ever seen her in such a state.

From what I have been able to find out, your decedent's name is Misha Kloski. He and his friends are Polish. They have no money. They are insistent that he is not to be cremated. We occasionally do charity cases, but rarely a burial. I gave them the best price I could, and they swore they would pay no matter what. He was under a doctor's care and died in a hospital. I'm not sure how long I can hold him. Why don't you let him sit a bit until we can figure this out?"

Two days later the little wagon pulled into the lot once again, followed by another large and very expensive foreign car. At the time I had no idea the occupants of both vehicles had something in common with Misha. All entered the office together. I stood idle a few minutes and then did not wait for a summons. I headed toward the office. Ed noticed me through the window and motioned that it was okay to enter. "Well, we might as well all move into the conference room." The spokesman translated for the others, and we were herded into the seldom-used room.

The man driving the expensive car was wearing a tailored sport coat, and he began the introductions. "I am Dr. Denton Bernard. I took care of Mr. Kloski the last few weeks of his life. The reason I am here is that he had a most unusual life and I have agreed to help his friends and family here, if I can."

The spokesman translated, and the room broke out in what sounded like so much gibberish. Those that surrounded the table spoke almost as fervently with their arms as they did with their mouths. It bordered on a danger zone, getting too near the swinging limbs.

Dr. Bernard began. "Misha was a tall, thin, handsome man who entered the United States via Ellis Island. He remembered looking at the Statue of Liberty and really believed all he had heard about attaining the American dream. He had been given enough money to make the passage, stay in a flop house, and eat for a few days."

The translator waved a handful of colored paper in the air. "Zloty," is all he said.

"Zloty is the Polish currency," the doctor informed us. "Misha was a grateful man. He really wanted no part of the American dream for himself; he just wanted to help people less fortunate. With no money and only a strong back, he felt he would wait a few days to regain his strength after the ocean voyage and then be fit for hard labor.

"He was not an idealist – far from it. He expected the worst from people, and he usually was not disappointed. However, he made a personal vow that he would not pay back in kind."

The conversation was translated to Polish as rapidly as possible, and Dr. Bernard was taking pains to speak slowly and carefully. At the last part of the statement, the women began to wail loudly. This would likely take a while.

"Several times, until he got a handle on American currency, he was short-changed in his dealings in exchanging money, and often from the very merchants from his homeland that he dealt with. He learned, usually the hard way, who the few honest storeowners were, and sought them out. He always looked at the bright side. There were many other Poles in the same situation, and at his urging, they traded laughter and stories for the day's disappointments.

"Every day he and his companions searched for work. They rarely found it. Misha advertised his strong back. He took to cutting wood, a day's work for a few meals. He and his friends pooled their resources. They barely made the rent. When the landlord noticed they made the rent, he raised it. Misha expected it and didn't complain. To him these small problems just did not matter. He was happy having new friends, a place to call home and good health."

He paused to let the translation catch up. Ed was not in a hurry, so I guess neither was I.

"Life went on. Misha worked odd jobs and always had a small, but steady income. As it is in such cases when people live together in close confines, Misha took ill one day and developed a cough that would just not go away. He laughed and was happy. After all, hard work would make it go away."

A man who kept silent until now put a fist in front of his mouth and made coughing noises. "Cough," was all he said, and smiled at us expectantly.

"That is Leyva," the Polish translator said. "He is learning English."

We smiled and nodded in praise of his new word. He beamed.

"Anyway," the doctor continued, "weeks later he was worse. He agreed, under protest, to go to the public health clinic. To him, the dingy, smelly, understaffed place was a bit of Heaven. Even in that, the health care was far and above better than what was available at home. He could sit in a comfortable office and be seen by a doctor for free. He had X-rays taken that very day. In his country, they were a luxury, reserved for the upper class.

"The X-rays confirmed the doctor's diagnosis. Misha had acquired tuberculosis and needed admission to the county hospital for evaluation and possible treatment. That is where I first met him. His attitude was incredible. He almost cried with joy when he told me how much he was enjoying American television, a clean bed, food and the visits from his friends. Compared to the sniveling and whining I have to endure from most of the patients I see, he was a saint.

"We offered Misha clean clothes, but he stubbornly clung to his long-sleeve undergarment. When we examined him, he would pull it up for us, but refused to take it off."

At this point in the story the ladies around the table broke into a fresh set of sobs. They all held an arm up and pointed to it, but we had no idea what the gesture meant.

The doctor shook his head slowly and touched one of their hands sympathetically.

"The fellow translating assures me we will understand their tears in a bit. Anyhow, one day Misha got a roommate. He was a very sick man. Every day people stood over the bed and whispered in hushed tones. Since the county hospital is also a teaching hospital, the foot traffic seemed endless. With each consult, and with each day, Misha would look at this poor man, and there would be another tube added, another medicine bottle hanging and another procedure the man might have to endure. The poor patient could not speak, but at times would let out an occasional moan which sent chills through Misha and caused him to have terrifying nightmares."

The self-proclaimed translator took over the story and spoke in broken English. Every few sentences he would translate, and at this point in the story his shoulders stooped and his face grew somber. Most around the table had already heard the story, and heads nodded and arms waved either in agreement or in embellishment, who could tell?

"Misha have nightmares. Misha look at man in bed, and Misha was very, very afraid. Every day Misha beg. He beg me, he beg everyone. 'I no die like that! No tubes! No machines!'"

As he translated, the crowd became the most animated I had seen. Wild gesticulating and loud clamoring ensued, as everyone tried to outdo the other. Soon, very soon, I would understand.

The translator became lost in his own frenzy of thought and words. Ed and I ceased to exist for the group while they, undoubtedly, recounted their own personal interactions with Misha. The doctor picked up the story again and the room quieted, hanging on his words.

"Misha's roommate was subjected to all that 'modern' medicine had to offer, and he died. Even after the man was removed from the room, you could still see the terror in Misha's eyes as he begged the staff to not allow him to die like that.

"One day a young doctor came in and informed him he would need an intravenous line for his medicines. Misha refused. The doctor pressed and Misha smiled and gave in. 'Okay just this one thing.'"

"Oh, and in case you haven't figured it out, that doctor was me."

As this portion of the translation ended, murmurings rumbled from the table. It was clear the doctor was not popular at this moment. His eyes darted about, but he continued as the translator shushed the crowd.

"Days later I came back in and told him we would need to hook him up to a machine to watch his heartbeat. He protested, but in the end, he gave in again. He told me more than once that he was having bad dreams, but I figured they were just him being in a strange place. He told me they were becoming more vivid, but I wasn't listening."

The man who prided himself on his tiny grasp of English spoke up. "Misha. Dream. No good." Then he translated for the crowd, which brought about another paroxysm of fervent chatter.

Dr. Bernard finished the story. "The more machines and tubes we used on Misha, the more tests we ran, the more panic and outright horror was present in his face. Misha never gave in, but we just kept adding more. After all, modern medicine always knows what's best." He almost spit out the sentence.

"Finally the day came and Misha needed this young doctor's help, even to breathe. Another machine, another tube."

A woman tugged on the sleeve of the translator's shirt, wanting to be heard. She spoke a few words directed to him, and she turned to the audience and said, "People of the old country, we not like hospitals. We visit Misha, but finally, no more."

The doctor added. "They never saw Misha in all the grand splendor that is medicine. All they knew is that he went into the hospital and never came out. A human being encased in a spider web. Tubes to eat, tubes to use the bathroom. Misha had a strong will, but it was ebbing, and he knew it. He took a piece of paper and wrote a note. He addressed it to me, 'The Young Doctor.' Then he reached over and pulled at every tube and machine he could, including the breathing tube. He died a quick, courageous death."

At the end of the translation, the translator stood up very slowly and somberly. He removed a note from his jacket pocket and unfolded it with great fanfare. He began reading the Polish words. *"Mlody Doktor: Boi Smierc nie sa wrog, To jest czlowek inhumanity do czlowieka."* (Young Doctor: Pain and death are not the enemy. It is man's inhumanity to man.).

Dr. Bernard stared at his hands and could not speak for a few minutes. The women cried softly. It was the first time anyone, including the doctor, had heard Misha's last words.

The doctor turned and addressed the crowd, shaken, and perhaps needing to do so as a catharsis. "I am a doctor. I made a terrible mistake that I will never make again. Mr. Kloski was one of my patients. Because he was obviously a foreigner, I assumed he did not understand what medicine was all about. I treated him the best I knew how. He fought me every step of the way. From now on I will listen to the wishes of the patients. I need their help to make them better."

The young translator spoke to the others, and it was evident he wanted them to stay put. The mood around the table seemed to soften a bit after the doctor's compassionate confession. The young man motioned to Ed, the doctor and me to follow him. He pointed to the garage and asked, "Misha stay here? Show me Misha."

I looked at Ed and he nodded. We pulled Misha out of the cooler and the young man came forward. "Please. Cut sleeve off shirt."

We did, and all the pieces of the last hours came together in a few seconds. Inside the left forearm were tattooed several numbers. The young man shook his head, and the doctor put his face in his hands. The young man explained, even though none was necessary.

"Treblinka. No other place worse. He survived ovens. I promise Misha, no oven, no burn. You no burn."

Ed spoke, and even though the young man's grasp of English was only rudimentary, Ed's words seemed to get through. "Treblinka was notorious for performing some of the most brutal, inhuman, and horrific experiments ever devised on living humans, and called it 'medicine.'

"The Japanese warlords of the seventeenth century killed quickly. The ruthless Mongols killed quickly. It was this century that spawned this madness."

From the corner where he sat brooding, the doctor added, "Misha's friends could never understand why he was always so happy. He had been imprisoned for six years. Six years of almost continuous torture, and then he had to die reliving it in the hell that modern medicine created for him."

Ed, the doctor, and the young man returned to the office. I stayed behind, content for the moment to sit and stare awhile, just Misha and me, alone with our thoughts.

*Was Misha at peace? Had he ever not been at peace? Did the brutality he had received automatically guarantee him a place in Heaven?*

I knew from this day forward that I would no longer complain bitterly if my latte wasn't hot enough, or if someone cut me off in traffic, or if I was short-changed a few cents.

I was contemplating these and other questions when Ed returned. "Dr. Bernard sat down and wrote out a nice check. He wants Misha to receive a proper casket burial. The young man who translated for us, told the doctor that at first, he thought he was quite a character. Now he knows that the young doctor has character.

I teach my children the truth about history. There are moments in time when mankind has given the earth a black eye, but I feel that learning truth, good or bad, may teach my kids that the bad is not worth repeating. I do not dwell on the ugly, but I have showed them pictures of Treblinka, Dachau, Auschwitz. They have asked me, "If it was so horrible, why doesn't someone tear these camps down? Why are these places allowed to stand?"

My answer? These places must stand to show the history of the earth when man walked about without a heart. He allowed the earth to become a grave. Into this grave he shoveled reason, sanity, logic, and worst of all, his conscience. I tell my children, if we don't have some sort of visual reminder of these horrors, mankind will forget, and once again, he will become a gravedigger.

# Chapter 8:
# A Child's Garden of Curses

What I have learned is that man's inhumanity to man can extend beyond the grave – frustration, anger and resentment that were not resolved in a lifetime are carefully orchestrated by the dying; so even in death, they can reach out with one last message of bitterness. The brunt is usually borne by a family member; more often than not, a parent. These are lessons that a dead man and his living father taught me.

Work was starting to show great promise. I was looking forward for the next nugget to arrive. When would the inner voice speak up again and say, "Stop here. Learn from this one"?

More and more I was arriving at work eager and expectant. I no longer looked at cremations as quick, simple and boring. Ed must have sensed it too, because he stopped "assigning" me cases he thought would be interesting to me. True, I received my share of interments and cremations, but he knew I would no longer need to be prompted to sift through them and glean some interesting tidbits.

Today it was my turn to cremate a decedent after a viewing, with the added stipulation that the cremation itself would be witnessed. This was not uncommon, as the relatives wanted assurance that their requests for their loved one were actually being met, and oddly enough, some wanted assurance that the "cremains" they were receiving in the urn were actually *their* beloved. The closed box was on the work table, and I opened it, and unzipped the shroud. Well! Here was something new!

The corpse was that of a man, late forties, or possibly fifty, and dressed head to foot in full clown's regalia, from the red rubber nose to the oversized "Bozo" shoes. His face was not painted and there was a nasty scar on his left cheek. I took a step back to survey the scene. Just what was I supposed to do with this?

Pinned to his flannel shirt was a note left by the attendant from the night before. There were written instructions:

"This man died in a trailer and was signed off by the coroner as a suicide. The instructions to the funeral home are the wishes of the decedent: use as much makeup as needed to keep this man looking like a clown, even in death. The more garish, the more macabre, the better. He will be viewed, then cremated."

I was at a loss as what to do next. There was no death certificate and no name. I would have to find the attendant and ask him at what facility the deceased had died. I sought Ed out and filled him in.

"No problem," he smiled, and leaned over to a file cabinet. "I think I can help you with the name and perhaps some of the history as well, if we get lucky. The last time the circus was in town, I met some of the performers. I keep in touch, occasionally."

I made a mental note to stop underestimating Ed. Was there anyone he did not know? He continued to amaze me by the people he counted as friends, the life-experiences he had but did not advertise and his talents. Years later, he can still catch me off guard. He would reveal a tidbit about himself that I had been unaware of, and all I could do was to leave and shake my head in awe. I will always wonder what other secrets Ed's file cabinet held.

*Hey Ed! I am sort of glad you took those files with you when you left. Those were your friends, your memories, and I am making my own. Was that where you kept the hearts and souls of all the people that meant so much to you? Did you turn to them for strength? Is that what made you so strong? Did the friends you made tell you of their pitfalls, their un-realized dreams? Is that how you grew and maintained yourself? Are you and your friends all up there reminiscing? In that file cabinet, Ed, is that where your values lie? Should I look for something deeper? Why did you empty the files and just leave a Bible behind?*

"There is a circus in town every year," Ed said. "It is a small, local affair. Most of the entrants live in the city. They build the circus and manage it for a few weeks out of the year because they love it. They are passionate about preserving its beauty and art. I know a few of them. Some of them were very big names before settling here." He handed me a card with a name and number. "The number on the card belongs to a man who is still a performing clown. Why don't you give him a call and see if he can be of help?"

Several moments later, I was on the phone.

A man answered. "Hello?"

"Hello. I am calling from Carson's Funeral home. Is Mr. Roy Harlan there?"

"Speaking! But I'm afraid you've gotten to me a bit early. I ain't dead."

I chuckled in what I hoped was an appreciative tone, but groaned inwardly. "I'm calling because I'm in a bit of a bind and Ed, my boss, thought you might be of help. We received a man here dressed in a clown suit. Not some cheap store suit, but very professional. Shoes and all. We should be able to identify him later today, but his next of kin is not being very helpful."

"Hmm. You say clown, huh? Hmm. Well it just so happens that I know Ed quite well, and I owe him a favor or two. What say you give me a day, and I'll drop by? Give me a good excuse to call on you folks."

I grasped at any chance of help, but did not want to sound too eager. "Well, I suppose that would be okay if you think you can help…"

"Son, if it has anything to do with a legitimate clown in a legitimate circus, if I don't know about it, I know someone who will."

"Great, then. I'll look forward to your visit."

I hung up and wandered back to the office. Ed was leaning on the desk talking with Donna, and he looked up. "So what did you find out?"

"Nothing much. Roy Harlan is coming tomorrow with some info. I'm not sure if it will help, but he seems to want to visit you."

"Well, now, that's fine. Roy is certainly one of the good guys and it will be great to see him again. Let's go see your man."

We retrieved the body and noticed something I had missed at first glance. Someone had placed a picture in his hand. It seemed to be him in full clown regalia, face paint and all. Ed scratched his head. "I think I know this man."

*Why am I not surprised to hear that?* I thought to myself.

"Mind if I sit in and chat with you and Roy?"

I chuckled. "Not at all. Should be interesting. Oh, by the way, you had better take this before I lose it." I handed him the card he had given me with Roy's name and number.

The next day I tried to plow my way through the mundane paperwork that always creeps into a job such as this. Ed saved me from part of the tedium, approaching me in the late afternoon. "You want to come over and meet Roy?"

I had to think for a moment. Oh, yes. Roy, who was going to solve the mystery of the clown. I stretched, yawned, and said, "Sure. Lead the way."

Seated in the conference room were three people. A tall man with a protruding Adam's apple stood up and introduced himself. He was Roy Harlan. Accompanying him was a short, balding man, cheery faced, and heavy. He smiled, and as he did so, he kept his mouth closed, but still his grin was literally, from ear to ear. He reminded me of a ventriloquist's dummy.

"Hi. I'm Benny Hill. I had my name legally changed to that of the British comic. He was my idol." His face did actually bear a physical resemblance to the famous comedian, but whether by design or intent, I could only guess.

Roy added. "Benny is a clown in our local circus. I am the ringmaster or announcer if you will."

Also at the table was a somewhat attractive middle-aged woman. Her mood was somber, reserved. "My name is Martha." That was all she said.

Ed passed the picture around and when it reached Martha, she looked up in horror and stifled a sob.

Ed spoke. "Roy thinks he might have a lead on your guy, but he brought Benny and Martha along for confirmation. Then addressing the three, "Would it be too difficult on any of you if we were to go visit our man?"

No one spoke, but they all rose and followed us to the prep room. I retrieved the man from the cooler and pulled the blanket off his face. Roy just shook his head and Martha took a deep breath and sighed. Benny looked up at us like a child who just skinned his knee and was trying to put up a brave front. What was registering on the faces and in the minds of the three, Ed and I had no clue. Ed broke the spell and suggested that we return to the office. All took one last long glance at the man in the box and then filed out of the room.

Once seated, Ed offered coffee, but all refused. Roy looked round the room and was the first to speak. "All of us are fairly sure that who you have here was one of the most famous clowns of the modern day circus. His name was Robert. Anyone familiar with the history of the modern day circus knows him as The Great Payaso."

Benny was nervous, and fidgeted. He told us that he, like most clowns, was more at ease performing in character than speaking in public. His voice fit his physique; high pitched and squeaky. "One of the reasons I stay active in circus events is because I got the rare privilege of having as a mentor, one of the greatest clowns I can think of. I do it for his memory. When I perform, the characters within me are Robert and myself, coming alive in a suit of lights. Being a clown, you see, is not just some inept buffoon fumbling around. It is a one-man play. It is an art. It is communicating the strongest language possible, the most fervent feelings, but never saying a word.

"When I am sad, it lets me express sadness, but the audience never knows. They pay to see the clown, I can give them their money's worth, no matter what I am feeling that day."

Martha to this point had been silent. She sat quietly, dabbing her eyes with tissues that were always at the ready in this business. "I guess if you want to know anything, I should start. I knew him the best socially, the others knew him professionally. He and I were lovers and confidants. I'm afraid I am not being very quick to discover that a broken heart cannot last forever. It was I who pinned that note to his shirt, and later you will see why."

She began Robert's story. "Robert was the son of a very staunch and legalistic preacher. The father's personality was such that, although he graduated from seminary and considered himself a Christian, he could never come to grips with Jesus' statement that Christians should be recognized by their love for one another. Furthermore, he never understood the Apostle Paul's emphasis on love. For him, it was all too abstract.

"He searched both the Old and New Testaments and discovered something more concrete: rules. He needed rules and busied himself pulling verses out of context to support this. Rules and legalism he could understand and he was convinced that this would help him to salvation. He further concluded that saving souls meant enforcing these rules rather than some vague passages about love, grace and forgiveness. He started with his family.

"He constantly admonished the entire family to behave accordingly: Keep laughing and smiling to a minimum. If you must eat with company, only have one helping. School grades must be high. Appearance was everything. The father made a good living, but he insisted on austerity. The mother and daughter must always wear modest skirts with high necklines. The father had several suits, all varying shades of gray. There were two sons,

Robert being the elder. Life's important lessons were duty and respect. After all, the mantle of the firstborn would fall on Robert. His life was already perfectly choreographed. Dad would send Robert to the conservative seminary he himself attended.

"Robert, however, had other plans. He exhibited all the traits his brother and his sister would not. He was outgoing, wild spirited, tall and very handsome." She emphasized the word "very" by drawing it out. She drummed her fingers on the table and thought a bit before she spoke again.

"His studies came easy for him. But divinity school? Fat chance. The more the father pressed, the more rebellious the son became. Robert suggested a compromise. Perhaps a year off to explore the world or consider his options, then school. His father adamantly refused. Robert went his own way, just the same. He was stubborn. As with so many people his age, he felt he knew more than adults did. So, explore he did.

Rumors of the actions of the handsome preacher's boy filtered back to the family. Nothing was ever substantiated, but trysts with girlfriends seemed to be the only logical explanation, at least in the father's eyes. For this family, sex outside marriage was anathema.

"One day, shortly after his nineteenth birthday, father and son confronted each other.

Robert wanted his father's love and approval. The father wanted to give it… as he understood it. "Live under his rules, or leave. Those are my conditions; that is what it takes to earn my love.'

"Robert chose to leave." Martha paused, visibly shaken.

Benny looked about, fidgeting and in obvious distress. Then he spoke.

"Robert's dad gave him a going-away present. 'Son,' he said, 'your good looks have always gotten you into trouble. Some day you will thank me for this.' With that, he brought his hand up quickly to Robert's face. Hidden in his palm was a small knife. Faster than Robert thought possible, his father laid open a three-inch gash in his cheek. Robert grabbed a towel to staunch the blood, and then walked out.

"The wound became infected and never healed properly. Robert never had it tended to. The scar healed, cruel and jagged. With his looks gone, his confidence waned. In his mind, he was hideous. He could not hold a job. One day, while working at a pizzeria geared to children, he saw a young boy and smiled at him. The child screamed, and ran off in tears. Robert loved children and vowed he would never let this happen to another child.

"Not long after this, the pizza shop was in need of replacing the employee in the clown suit that walked the floor entertaining the patrons. He applied and was accepted. At first, he wore the standard cheap suit and performed the usual antics. He was ecstatic. People appreciated him and did not shy away from him. He took great pains to cover the scar with thick makeup. His outfits became more outlandish, his face paint more creative. His audience loved him."

Roy raised his hand to interject, and Benny sat back in his chair as Roy resumed the story. "The circus was in town and we posted our flyers. We weren't looking for a clown, but he was passionate about a tryout, and we gave him a shot. He was very good. Quite gifted, and a natural. He was an instant success. People came expecting to laugh, and laugh they did.

He threw himself into every performance. We told him we would like to bill him as The Great Payaso. When we told him the name was the Spanish word for Clown, and there was even an Italian opera about his namesake, he had tears of pride. We put "The Great Payaso" on the marquee, in lights. He was the big draw.

"Robert spoke a lot about his 'dark side,' and attributed most of it to his family. I really didn't notice this too much in him, just that he would occasionally give in to bouts of depression. But as soon as the suit was on, he was transformed into a performing genius. I suggested he see a psychologist. He told me that at the second visit, the doctor thought he was just 'sad,' and told him that the circus was in town and he had gone and laughed at the clowns. He recommended that he too, go see the clowns"

Martha seemed to have collected a second wind, and she quickly started up again before Roy had a chance to continue. "We traveled through many states and finally we managed to play near his hometown. In a rare display of generosity and totally out of character – at least in Robert's mind – his father, mother, and siblings made it to a performance, not knowing their family member was top billing. Although they had not seen each other for years, as soon as the clown came on, there was no doubt in the father's mind the Great Payaso was his son.

"After the performance, the father followed him back to his motor coach. The reunion was both pleasurable and painful. Robert cried and forgave his father. The father cried and begged Robert to return home. He promised things would be different, but he hoped that Robert would quit the circus. Robert wanted to go back, he craved the father's love, but it was still conditional. Don't you see? He loved the circus and loved being a clown. In his clown ego, he could be anyone he chose. He could act any part. His father could not understand, and left with bitterness in his voice. He spit out a parting malediction 'If this clown suit makes you happy, may you be buried in it.' They would never see each other again.

"Ironically, as Robert sank deeper into depression, the more his brilliance emerged, and the crowds grew."

The ringmaster sighed deeply and his voice took on a melancholic air as he picked up the story. "A good clown craves the sound of laughter from all ages, but it was the children that Robert loved the most. At the end of his shows, he would approach the children in the front rows and pour a bucket over their heads and out would come glitter. The kids roared, after realizing there was not the expected water. Robert would fetch an oversize paintbrush and make a pretense of sweeping off a bit of glitter from someone's shoulders. One night, he forgot the brush and had to improvise. In front of hundreds, he brushed off glitter from the sweater of a little girl. The mother was horrified and accused him of inappropriate behavior.

"What could I do? I wanted to save the circus, and I let him go."

Martha finished the story. "At first I was furious with Roy. Another spineless human being who stood for nothing and allowed political correctness gone terribly awry to dictate his morality."

She glared at Roy as she said this. Clearly, she had not forgotten or forgiven. "I mean, this was witnessed by hundreds of people. But perhaps it was for the best. Robert had been pushing himself past his limits, and it was beginning to show. He lived in his motor home on the property, but after that he was never the same.

"A few weeks after the incident, we found Robert, my friend, my confidant, the Great Payaso, dead by his own hand. On prominent display and taped to the dresser mirror a note read, 'Dear Father. You got what you wanted. Now give me what I want. Please bury me as a clown.

To the mortician: Fix my makeup to show anger, bitterness, and pain.'"

Ed had been silent the whole time, and said aloud to no particular person, "Hence the picture."

Roy spoke up again. "Perhaps we could be of help? Could we pay our last respects by fixing him up according to his wishes?"

Benny and Martha looked at each other in surprise. After a moment of thought, they accepted the idea gratefully. Ed looked at me, hands open in indecision. "It's your case, you decide."

I nodded my head in assent. "Sure. Why not. A most fitting passage for a clown."

The three volunteers subjected Robert to an eerie transformation. They painted fear and sorrow on his face. They concealed the facial scars with a symmetrical pattern drawn on each cheek. They hid the scars on his body, but I wondered, would the fires of the crematory be hot enough to burn out the scars on his soul?

Over the course of the next 48 hours, a trickle of visitors showed, all from the circus. Finally, the day of the cremation arrived, and Robert had his last visitor. A dour-faced man in a gray suit shuffled in slowly, shoulders stooped. He stayed in the viewing room and then approached me. He identified himself simply as "Robert's father." He requested permission to witness the cremation and I obliged. Once I had placed Robert and began the automatic sequence, I exited the area and allowed him his privacy.

Over the course of the next hour, it was difficult for me and others to keep our ears shut to the cacophony that took place. The father screamed, swore, and begged of his son. He sobbed loudly for a bit, but then the tirade would start again. There was a period of silence, and the father finally emerged, head and shoulders low, and as silent as was possible, left.

Two major issues confronted me with this case. As a funeral director we have to deal with the despair and the guilt of families burying a loved one who has committed suicide. They come to us with the hard questions. Death and its accompanying grief is bad enough, but what about those who believe in an afterlife? Is suicide the unforgivable sin? Can a loving God forgive even this? Can a person who claims to be a Christian still make it to their Heaven if they take their own life?

I wonder if Robert knew that this would cause further anguish to his father the preacher. Years later, Adelina taught me that in her Bible, her God forgives all sin except for those that flat out continuously reject Him. She told me that there were stories in the Bible where people had killed themselves, but she was sure they were in Heaven. I am sure Ed thought the same thing. He would tell me often that good "Christian" people err, but the only difference was that they had a Comforter, an Advocate that would forgive them. Was the "sin" of suicide committed by a Christian any different than the "sin" of stealing? Lying?

Robert's goal had been to cause his father bitterness and despair beyond the grave. His father's goal was to dangle love as he understood it, just tantalizingly out of reach. Had they both lost?

I thought of Robert and his father a lot when I was raising my kids. I thought of the Alford's. I thought of Billy Jameson. Parents struggling to do their best by their children, but in the end, the best gift they had to offer was everlasting; that of unconditional love. What the child chose to do with it was anybody's guess.

Would the Alford's learn that love was more important than possessions?

Would Robert's father learn that you can't put love in a box and only open it up as a reward for obedience?

Hindsight is 20/20. I learned valuable lessons after my children were grown that I should have put into practice when they were young. Perhaps it is not too late. Perhaps they can pass the lessons my dead friends who, in their agony, taught me to remember in raising children: *Children are not yours. You are entrusted with them for a time, but only because their longing to find their own way in life draws them away from you too soon. Give them gifts that never wear out, never grow old. Give them your unconditional love, but not your thoughts and desires.*

Their bodies live in your house. Their souls are restive…always searching for their own place.

Be like them, if you wish, but don't try to make them be like you, because life is always moving somewhere, but it doesn't ever move backward.

Most importantly, you are the archer; they are the arrows. The Maker who made the archer and the arrows loves both. Let Him string the bow, let Him set them on their way.

# Chapter 9:
# I Dance and I'm not Happy, I Dance and I'm not Free

This is a story of Tammy, a young single mother who lost a child but gained a new spirit. Later I would meet a decedent named Louis Felan who lost a daughter but gained her heart. Ed must have known when he gave these two cases to me that there was still some vestige of the "old" Michael that had to surrender fully to love. The cost was high but the rewards were endless. Paying love's high price was the only way I could have ever held on to a mate like Adelina. These two cases are connected.

I am at the crypt, sitting with her. I know I could never love someone again as much as I loved her. Since her death, it could be argued that I am anti-social, much like I was before I met her. Not really, it's just that socializing with women just doesn't hold the fascination that it did when we were young and learning about each other.

*You know, my love," she was saying, "I married you with cautious optimism. I loved you unconditionally, you loved me with reservation. You wore a mask, and when it finally came down I saw fear. Fear of being in love. Fear of heartbreak.*

"Yes," I sighed. "I remember some of our conversations. You thought we should wait to have kids until I was ready to take chances.

Ready to fail. Ready to be vulnerable. I remember when I first came to Carson's and Ed lambasted me over the Thomas case, not because of the job I did, but how I reacted to criticism. I was cold and withdrawn and I wanted to remain impenetrable."

"And you told me that there is no insurance against heart break.

"And you told me that even the highest, most perfect love could not prevent pain. Children were a frightening concept. To love them, to love anything, is to be vulnerable. Love, and your heart will be wrong, and possibly even be broken. I wanted to make sure I kept mine intact. Do you remember how hard it was for me to even let the kids have a dog, knowing that I would eventually be responsible for its death no matter how peaceful we could make it?

"Before I met you, I thought I was comfortable. I had my heart wrapped around hobbies and food and other inane luxuries. I threw it in the caskets of some of my deceased friends. Emma Jean was probably laughing at my selfishness. But in those dark caskets… safe and airtight… it could not change. It could not be broken, because to suffer and to love are two sides of the same cloth and I was too weak to face either."

*But,* Adelina broke in, *that heart cannot be redeemable either. Couldn't you see that the alternative to risking a broken heart is damnation? Babe, you always told me one of your favorite books was Goethe's* Faust. *Remember what saved Dr. Faust in the end? Remember what the theme of the last few pages was?*

"Yes. That the only place outside Heaven where one can be perfectly safe from all the problems love can cause is Hell."

*Okay, Michael. So tell me again the stories of Tammy and her daughter; of Louis Felan and a broken heart; of those that threw away their defensive armor and allowed God to break their hearts so He could mend them in His way.*

I love my children but I am no good at loving someone else's. I don't like dealing with a dead child. The thought of my children preceding me in death terrifies me. Death may be preordained, but it doesn't mean we have to accept the timing. If mourning can be quantified, is there more profound grief over the loss of a child than of an eighty year old?

This was yet another question I posed to Ed, another question with no answer.

Long ago, I came to my own conclusions. Etched solidly in granite. In this day and age of disposable families, disposable parents, who will mourn for the castaway child? the abused? the neglected? What about children born with horrible defects? Are they loveable? If they cannot accept love, if they are unable to feel emotion, does giving them love become a waste of time?

Perhaps we mourn so earnestly the death of a young child because this world can ill afford to lose the innocence they bring so unashamedly. They have not yet learned pretentiousness and hypocrisy.

So the day came. It was my turn. Ed gave me the file. I was to prepare for cremation a young girl named Tammy. I tucked the folder under my arm and sighed. Children were never easy. Death was almost never the result of "natural causes."

I pulled Tammy out from the cooler and folded the sheet back, steeling myself to not react. And I saw a woman, about thirty years old. I checked the file. This was indeed Tammy. The date of birth matched. I sat down to review the file more closely. Ed, always in tune with his staff, must have known I would have questions. He appeared, looking over my shoulder as I was lost in thought. Nothing he did surprised me much anymore. Ed was a man who listened, heard and responded to that still, small voice that most can't hear.

I looked up and smiled. "I thought I was getting a child," I said.

"Well," he began, "if you search hard enough, you might just find a child in this case. Perhaps later as you do young children here, it might go easier on you, perhaps not. This case may ease your way. Some directors just don't function well around youngsters and I don't force the issue. I'm giving you this as a teaching case, because if you can handle this one, I think you will be well-equipped to handle just about anything that comes your way. Do your homework."

With that he was gone.

So I did my homework. I met Tammy's mother. I met a few people who came to pay their last respects. We reconstructed the last few days of her life.

Tammy woke up at 6:30 a.m. No longer in need of an alarm clock, she had been waking up at 6:30 for years. She wanted to get up and tend to the needs of her baby before the little girl stirred. Quietly she made her way to the kitchen and prepared coffee for herself, formula for her daughter. She went into the child's room and fed her and changed her. She fed her through a tube, placed in her stomach long ago. She looked down at the child, almost 4 years old, unable to talk coherently, unable to walk, and who would never be able to be potty-trained.

But, when the little girl smiled, none of that seemed to make a difference. When she smiled, Tammy knew it was going to be a good day.

Fast-forward in time a few years. The little girl is almost 10 now. Tammy's routine has not changed in the least, but for the times when her own mother would come to give her a few hours of respite.

Tammy's life to this point would have dismantled most people. Her husband left her during her pregnancy. The marriage had lasted only six months. In the ten years that followed, her father died after lingering in a coma for years. She loved her father. He was there in good times and bad. She would constantly ask him why he did what he did, why he never turned his back on her and never chided her for bad choices. Why did he love her unconditionally, even when it was so hard to do? He would always pause, look at her and smile, and say, "The day you were born I looked at your beautiful face and gave my word to you I would never leave you. A promise is a promise."

Her mother could not help with medical bills, but was always available to give Tammy a break from the tedium.

Today Tammy's mom was coming. Together they would begin the arduous task of bundling the daughter and all her tubes and special diapers together, somehow get her situated into the car and go shopping. But it was not just another shopping day; they were planning a tenth birthday party for a little child who had no idea why a birthday was any different than any other day. Nine times in the past she had a birthday... a day she did not know, a day she could not comprehend.

The little girl gave her mom a big smile. There was a twinkle in her eyes. Tammy went to the kitchen to get her coffee.

When she came back, the child was dead. The little girl's mother sobbed and sobbed. Tears of frustration, tears of... well, everything but rage. She was a bit envious. Now she was alone. Her daughter was in a place where she could walk, talk, laugh, play, but now Tammy had to face the unknown, an uncertain future, all by herself.

She was still crying when her mother came in. They both sat and cried together for a time. Then they did what had to be done.

After the child was gone from the house, there was work to do. Assuring her mother that she would be all right by herself, Tammy went about her usual daily routine.

Before her marriage, Tammy had a bit of a crush on a boy named Timmy. So when her husband left her, she resurrected an old

45 record by a group called "Destiny" whose lead singer was also named Tim. She would play side "A," an upbeat tune called "My Destiny," and dance around her daughter's play pen... every day. Her dance was almost a language they could both understand. It connected them, and the little girl smiled and blew little contented bubbles. At nine years of age, still with a pacifier in her mouth, her daughter smiled. Today would be no different. She turned on the music, but she couldn't dance.

Family photos taken to the funeral home where the daughter had been taken showed a radiant Tammy.

"All I wanted," she said, "was a little girl, and God granted me my wish."

The little girl was born perfectly. She cooed, ate, and smiled. Tammy looked down on her the day of her birth and vowed she would never leave her, never stop loving her, no matter what the cost. When the child was a month old she went into the nursery and found her unresponsive in her crib. She tried mouth-to-mouth and was successful in reviving her. She rushed to the hospital, the child on her lap. She shook the little girl occasionally to keep her from falling asleep, desperately willing her to live.

Live she did. Tammy brought her home, eyes sparkling, a tube in her stomach for feeding, legs that would never carry her, and the eyes of a mother who would look down on this child and every day say, "A promise is a promise."

The child was embalmed and presented for viewing. Tammy rarely left the funeral home and sat by her side for hours, holding her hand. The viewing area around her was transformed. There were angels, hand-cut from white paper with silver glitter sprinkled on their wings, hanging from the ceiling. A music box played. Framed pictures of family and pets adorned the area. Stuffed animals kept a close eye out.

Even in death, Tammy had, what she herself called, a mystery of faith. She wanted to wait by the dead child's side until she was assured her little girl was being taken care of by someone who was as good a caregiver as she had been. She had always insisted that taking care of her daughter was a blessing from God, and that anyone who cared for her would in turn, be blessed.

A few days later the funeral director put his arm around Tammy and told her that the only person who could take care of her daughter as well she did was God. Tammy burst into tears and left to go see her mother. For the first time since the death of her daughter her mother thought she could see a breakthrough. Tammy was starting to grieve, as people do.

The following morning Tammy woke, again without benefit of an alarm clock. She fixed coffee for herself and formula for her daughter. She was finally ready to bury her little girl. It wasn't until the following day that she was found – dead – slumped by her daughter's bed. Toxicology, trauma, all blood tests came back negative.

Ed showed me the reports, the cause of death. He sighed and summed up the case.

"There is not a medical examiner alive who can diagnose a broken heart."

So why do I relay this story? Love is a spectrum of emotions – amazingly ecstatic, agonizingly painful. I still do not like taking care of children. Their spirit never dies. They can never be forgotten. The impact they have on people who never even knew them can be uplifting, and yet devastating. The death of a child changes a person and some of us resist change.

So much of this story I was unaware of, but Ed filled in the last piece. "You can go to the funeral home across town now. Tell them they can bury the baby girl. Then, and only then, can you cremate the mother."

After finalizing arrangements with the funeral director in charge of the little girl, I went to the store and bought a baby doll. I placed its hand in Tammy's hand. Her eternity in her heaven, her reward, would be to run, sing, and laugh hand in hand with her daughter.

The crematory hummed, I cried, and did not resist the change.

*I remember, Michael,* Adelina cooed from above, *You were changing and I loved you all the more.*

# Chapter 10:

# Imagine There Is a Heaven

I was sitting again with Adelina, discussing Tammy's case and telling her what a profound sense of well-being I have that our two children were physically normal and for the most part, mentally well-adjusted. I was telling her that I thought it should be a heavenly mandate from a merciful God that all children should be able to start out life with a fair shot... at least with no physical handicaps.

Then I started on a rant that she had heard so often, which was continuing to be a stumbling block for me as to why I as yet couldn't fully embrace her "Heaven."

*If a merciful God does exist, why does he allow the innocent to suffer? Why does he allow man, who He created, to wreak such havoc on his fellow man? Plagues? Famine? Evil?*

Adelina had tried to answer many times and I would never listen.

But now, sitting here with her and thinking of past conversations, I couldn't help wondering if she had been right all along. I hoped for her sake she was.

I thought of her words, *What if God promised a Heaven, achieved so easily and without pain, here on earth. Heaven would not seem too much of a prize, would it? Think of yourself, Michael, how you are always so angry against the injustices of the world, yet you want to stay here? If the world was as you wished it to be, then what reason would there be to test your sincerity and faith? Why would you need Heaven?*

*Don't you see? Without a cost, achievements are worthless. If something is achieved easily, is it of any worth? If there is no glimpse into Hell, then there isn't a Heaven. You think the world is in bad shape now, think what it would be like with no accountability, no longing for a better place. Can you imagine what evil would be like then? We would be no better off than beasts of prey... actually, they would be better than we are. They kill and eat when they are hungry; they don't kill or maim and leave carcasses strewn all about around just for sport.*

*Without obstacles, without misfortune, what pleasure would Heaven be? But these small misfortunes are proof of the existence of a loving God. As for what mankind does to each other, we cannot blame Him; we must blame ourselves and do our time, and thank Him that we are not immersed in this earth any longer than we are.*

So I re-played this talk we had in my mind and thought, *I bet there is a mother and a little girl who are feeling the same way right now, and are thankful... that is, if they are not too busy running, laughing, and playing hand in hand.*

I promised that you would meet Louis Felan, and soon you will, but I find it odd that talk of Heaven seems to be reserved for dead people and funerals. Is that really a place worth striving for? Is there a worse alternative? I always thought that if Heaven were real, it would be reserved for "good" people like Tammy and her daughter, and Louis and his daughter, but take a moment with me to listen to Dan's story, because if Dan made it to Heaven, then there may be hope for all of us.

My friends, living and dead, hold me accountable. I sense "eyes" on me constantly. What they require of me, as a fee for lessons they teach, is that I must give back somehow. For my colleagues and my family I must be mature, slow to judge, and quick to pass on the invaluable lessons I am learning.

Unfortunately, I cannot do this by myself. I seek strength of character among the wealthy, the intellectual and the working class. Ed told me many times that I cannot maintain an air of calm and inner strength all by myself, because by myself I can do nothing. He is right. But if that's the case, how does he get through the trials of his day? If I had reserves of integrity and morality, how would I teach that to others? To my children? I remember that Mrs. Jameson said a man would do well to pass kindness and quiet confidence to his mate. How does one attain that? Where is it? Once it is found, how is it kept?

Surely Dan, a 300-pound-biker along with all his riding friends would in no way be able to help me fill in these gaps.

My children ask me if I believe in Heaven. I tell them yes, but it is the sort of a "yes" response you give to a child when they ask you if there is a Santa Claus.

I used to think of Heaven as a crutch. Now, I'm leaning toward the thought that perhaps it is indeed, a reality. For that I have Adelina, Ed, Dan and his friends to thank.

One morning at work, Carson's presented me with one of the largest men I had ever laid eyes on, even to this day. All I knew about him so far was that his name was Dan and he was a coroner's case. Already released to Carson's, he would have a viewing and then be cremated. He was a bearded giant, 6' 7", 340 pounds, and he barely fit the exam table lengthwise. Rolls of fat draped over the sides. He had died a day earlier and still had signs where the hospital had tried in vain to prolong viability. Dan was big, ugly and slovenly, so I guessed that few, if any, people would show to pay their last respects.

Oh. Did I mention earlier that whenever I made snap judgments about people I was usually wrong?

I was surprised to hear I could expect twenty-five or so people at the viewing. Preparation was quick and easy. We dressed him in his black leather jacket and a cloth cap that bikers called a "do-rag."

I'm flipping through Dan's file so many years later. I remember that day, finishing up with him and he laughed at me and made me promise to tell his friends that they didn't have to worry about him getting mixed up with a little guy in a red suit and a pitch fork. I had no clue of what he was talking about until the end of his story.

The following morning, it was business as usual until about ten o'clock. Then something could be heard that made many pause and look about. It sounded like thunder, but the sky was clear. We didn't have long to wait and wonder. Dozens of bikers, all clad in black, some two to a bike, most astride deep-sounding, huge, rumbling Harleys stampeded into the parking lot.

They came in and asked to see Dan. I escorted them, somewhat tentatively, into the viewing room. They circled about, gawking wordlessly, many moved to tears. Somehow, they all managed to cram themselves into the small space. The doors stayed open to allow some to spill out into the office. A small man about fifty or so stood on a chair and motioned for quiet. Surprisingly, the unruly crowd obeyed.

I hung back, curious, and found out that his name was Skip. He was a chaplain of sorts for a rival biker group, but members of several different groups had assembled at this time for a common purpose. The patches on his jacket, like the others present, had Christian themes.

All were putting their philosophical differences on hold for the day. I decided my work could wait and stayed to listen. My prejudices once again seeped to the surface and got the better of me. What could this rag-tag assembly offer in the way of spiritual care and comfort? Why bother with this bunch anyway? And, of course, I would be wrong yet again.

Skip opened with a short prayer. I was surprised to see everyone remove headgear, and all bow heads. After a lusty round of "Amens," he began telling Dan's story.

"For those of you who didn't know Dan, he was never as happy as when he was leading his pack to another ride, another rally. He was fiercely loyal. Bright, too! Just not well-educated. It didn't matter. I am sure there are those here who can assure us Dan could out-drink or out-fight anybody. But is there anyone here who wasn't glad to have him around?" There were snickers, murmurs, and head nodding all around.

"He told some pretty wild tales, and I doubt there was anyone here who would challenge the truth of those stories." More chuckling.

"We all take pride in our patches and our tattoos. Dan took pride in his lack of teeth and his scars.

"I met up with Dan a few months ago at a rally where my group was in charge of doing a church service Sunday morning. After Saturday nights at rallies, we are never sure of what kind of turnout we can expect, or if most of you guys can shake the cobwebs out of your heads long enough to understand what we are saying anyway. One day, Dan was at one of these services. Afterwards I got the nerve to approach him and asked him what he thought of the preaching and he told me he hated it. He was confused. How could you have fun and peace without drinking or fighting? Why did the Christian bikers have bikes just as nice as the outlaw bikers did? Just what did they have to offer that he would want, if anything? All of those "'Christian'" bikers looked tough enough, so what separated them from the hard-core outlaw groups?

"Heck, he had a good point. Who here cannot remember how you acquired the scars you have? The tattoos? The missing teeth?

"Dan complained bitterly that one of these Christians tried to convince him there was a place called Hell. They asked him if he would he be there after he died. He slapped me on the back in what I hoped was a friendly gesture, and told me, 'I ain't afraid of nothing. Especially a little man in a red suit with a pitchfork. If I go to Hell, so what? I'll be king.'

"I asked Dan if he remembered what he had heard during the Sunday service and he repeated it to me almost word for word. I tell you, Dan was no dummy.

"These were his words, as close as I can remember. 'Perhaps after we die we will end up in a big waiting room near the entrance to Heaven. We will wait and wait. Soon, an angel will open a door and call out a name. That person will jump up and raise their hand and say, "Here!" and get to enter a place where (supposedly), there is no anger, no fear, no pain, no sorrow; no more looking over your shoulder in distrust. But it may be another angel, one who comes out and stands in front of a person and shakes his head sadly and says "I'm sorry," and leads you to another door to an eternity of endless suffering, torment and shame.'

"Dan assured me he would have none of that nonsense. However, in light of the events of the last few days, I think there are others here who can better fill in the rest of the story. Suffice it to say that Dan and I kept in touch."

He got down off the chair and motioned to another man who made his way to the front. "Hi. I'm Chris, the road captain. As some of you may know, we were headed to a big three-day rally. The road and weather were perfect, and Dan was leading, as usual. We were rounding a turn and a truck crossed the centerline and hit him head on" At this point he stopped to compose himself. "Dan and his bike shot up, then crashed to the pavement. The rest of us stopped and it seemed everyone called 911 at once. At the hospital we were surprised to learn that he was still alive. The doctors told us it was real serious, and he was not expected to make it through the night. He ended up in intensive care hooked up to all sorts of machines. There was a tube coming out of his mouth to help him breathe. We took shifts, two of us at a time, sitting at either side of the head of the bed, never leaving. Whether he stayed on this earth or not, he was going to have the support and encouragement of his friends."

He clenched his fist and his voice took on a defiant tone. "If the nurses tried to tell us to leave, we told them in no uncertain terms we were here until he left, on foot or otherwise." This was met with hoots and applause.

Skip raised his hands and quieted the crowd. "Debbie? Weren't you and Jeff the last two with him?"

Two other bikers moved forward. The girl spoke. "Dan surprised everyone. He lived through the first night... then the next night. Me and Jeff were there that morning, like about three o'clock. All of the sudden he moved his head and opened his eyes. We got real scared. He looked around and raised his hand. He was trying to talk through the tube. We bent closer to hear. With his hand up, both of us heard the same thing. He said, "'Here,'" then he fell back and died."

The room fell silent but for a few sobs here and there. I was totally taken with this powerful message from these "simple" people, although I didn't agree or understand a lot they had to say at the time.

*Would I ever learn?*

*Hey, Dan; Hey, Skip. I learned, but it took years.*

The makeshift service ended and the bikers filed out. Many of them shook my hand and stayed around to talk. Some invited me to upcoming meetings. What an incredible awakening! They esteemed me as one who took good care of their friend and they accepted me. I had stayed to listen, and Skip told me that gesture meant a lot. Skip also told me that that was what Christianity was all about. Acceptance with no strings attached.

*Okay.* I thought. *Whatever.*

Others nodded, in effect saying "You're okay by us."

I watched as they roared off. Everyone involved with Dan's passing experienced a life-changing experience of some sort because a dying man shared an epiphany that was manifested in only a second, but would last them a lifetime... or perhaps even into eternity.

I went back to prepare Dan, and a few minutes later I heard the sound of one lone bike returning. It was Skip.

"Could I have his jacket?" he asked.

We cremated Dan minus his jacket, but sporting his do-rag.

I had always hoped to run into Skip again. As time went by it seemed to me that his was a piece of unfinished business, and I would need to take the initiative here. Finding him proved easier than I had hoped.

I took to the streets on a day off, and watched for motor-cyclists. I waved them to a stop as I encountered them. I kept doing this and on the fourth try I got lucky. The biker told me of the organization Skip belonged to and where they would meet. It was a restaurant in town.

I dropped by and asked a cashier about the meeting, and she told me the group had reservations a few nights from then.

I arrived at the appointed time, a few minutes early. I almost welcomed the familiar smell of sweat and leather. Skip was surrounded by people making small talk, and surprisingly, they were all drinking sodas. He noticed me but I don't believe he recognized me. I finally succeeded in getting his attention and pulling him to a secluded, less noisy spot.

After I re-introduced myself and small pleasantries were out of the way, I told him I really believed that I had a message from Dan for him. "Hey, Skip," I relayed, "tell the others. I never had to worry about the little guy in the red suit with his pitchfork!"

Even tough, old bikers can cry.

He invited me to stay for dinner and share Dan's story. Maybe next time.

# Chapter 11:

# Love and Other Acts of Bravery

I doubt if the question of whether or not my children learned anything from me will be answered in this life. Perhaps they learned from my wife, and if they told me she was the source of their morals, I wouldn't care, so long as they learned. Well… perhaps I would care a bit. Every human needs to feel that they have made an impact.

I think it was Walt Whitman who said something like "…that life is a powerful play and it must go on… and that you contributed a verse."

Soon you will make your own decision, because you will meet Louis Felan and his daughter. My experience with Tammy began the change in me as a father, and as to how I began to look at people. Those who I once perceived as hopeless, poor, and destitute were now people with stories to tell. They acquired strengths that I would never be able to attain.

I still don't particularly care to interact with the homeless people who stare me down on the street corners trying to gain my sympathy, but it was a homeless man who introduced me to a new concept. One may never know what impact they made in the life of another, but more often than not, people are surprised to learn how a powerful lesson can be taught with small actions, small words, by mediocre people... the value of encouragement. The man who taught me this was homeless most of his life.

I was preparing the man in front of me for a church service and a burial. It was a huge burden off my shoulders that I no longer needed to count my interments against those of my fellow workers to bolster my flagging self-worth. I was confident in how I did my job. My boss was confident in my ability and I no longer felt the need to run to him for self-assurance.

Raymond Mason, the deceased, was a non-descript man about sixty. In most cases, he would be termed a "nerd." He had a round face, horn-rimmed glasses, and a pasty complexion. I was, I had to admit, a bit taken aback when I was introduced to his wife when she came in to make the arrangements. She was beautiful. Gorgeous. It was a natural beauty, not made up. She was arrayed in expensive clothes and even more expensive jewelry.

What made her all the more attractive was almost mystical. She didn't flaunt her looks or her attire. She had an air of humility about her, along with the strain on her face that conveyed genuine grief. She was soft spoken and very polite. This was most definitely a case I would have to look into!

She had hoped for a small funeral, nothing too lavish, but she was a bit embarrassed to tell me that we could possibly expect several hundred people at the service.

I found time to chat with Ed in his office about the case.

"Oh, yes," he began. "You are taking care of Raymond Mason. He is a bit of a celebrity in the city. He leaves behind a wife and a little girl. Well, the little girl is not so little; I believe she is in her late teens, early twenties."

"The wife said we could expect quite a few mourners."

"Hmm…" he said as he scratched his head and thought. "Well, you'll probably get a good history if you are interested. All I know about the man is what I read in the papers awhile back."

So Ed had given me a good place to begin. The wife had definitely stirred my interest and I began to search for information in earnest. A few days later, after a search under Raymond's name, I was armed with copies of the local paper with some articles dating back twenty-five years. I had newspapers spread out on the tables, and some even piled on Mr. Mason when Ed entered the prep room with a stranger.

"This is Liam Nelson, a pastor of one of the local churches. Ray and his family attended there and Liam is handling the services. He has known Ray personally for years."

Pastor Nelson was not squeamish at the sight of Raymond, and he stared at him for a bit. He stayed close to the man while I made small talk and turned the pages of the newspapers, hunting for more articles. "Perhaps I can fill in some blanks for you, if you would like," he offered.

"Please!" I said. "I need some place to start. May I get you a cup of coffee?"

His shoulders relaxed and he took on a very casual air. He was a big man and we attained a pleasant rapport rather quickly.

"Yup. I can always use a good cup of strong black coffee, no matter where it comes from." He looked about the prep room, seemingly not too uncomfortable, but I assured him I would be right back. He seemed more at ease, now that he knew there was no coffeemaker in the same room with the deceased!

Coffee in hand and with me flipping papers, we spent several hours piecing together the story of a beautiful life. Pastor Nelson narrated:

"Raymond Mason entered the world naked, and spent most of his life homeless. He never begged for a handout, just relying on luck to carry him to the right places at the right time, finding a menial job, a few bucks, whatever. When he exited the world, the mayor wanted to pay for an expensive suit... from worldly rags, to Heaven's riches. The governor even called his wife to pay his respects.

"Raymond was a good kid, normal in every way, including average intelligence. The only thing not in his favor was his looks. He had a round, fat face on a lean body. He had hair, but it always looked like it had been added as an afterthought. No matter how it was cut or combed, it seemed that his head sprouted through like a turnip breaking soil. His looks caused no end of delight to crass people that didn't know better. He swallowed a lot of meanness from his peers, in high school and even as an adult."

I glanced at the body as Pastor Nelson spoke. I hadn't really paid much attention to Raymond's looks before this point, but now I was noticing more as the pastor narrated.

"He was fortunate to have a few close friends who accepted him for who he was. I have all too much experience with children not being accepted by their peers on the basis of some ridiculously trivial thing, but too often, it is enough to drive the poor child to suicide. Not Ray. I only wish that I could have half the strength of character he showed. His kind of strength cannot be found in a seminar.

"Through junior high and high school he found one teacher who taught him as he had never been taught. I remember, because later, I also was a student of Mr. Vogel. He was really an odd teacher and I remember at the time just wanting to get through his class. He was so weird. Most of us students dreaded the thought of taking a class from him, but looking back, I can't remember anyone who influenced me then and now like Mr. Vogel. Raymond was just more astute than the rest of us, I guess.

"I was fearful of the rumors I heard, that Vogel was stern, harsh, and gave impossible exams. The rumors proved to be true. When I became his student, he had been teaching for 25 years. Raymond preceded me by at least ten years. While I daydreamed through his class, Raymond absolutely thrived.

"Clarence Vogel taught English, writing skills, and literature. When I was his student, he was a few years from retirement. Why he stuck around as long as he did was anyone's guess. You could almost feel the daily resentment from the students in his classes. Raymond and I would wonder how this man could stand in front of class and almost willingly subject himself to the jabs and sneers he had to know were directed at him.

"But for those like Raymond, who listened as he read the droll, archaic literature in class, it came alive. Mr. Vogel showed them how it could apply to their lives for the present and the future, if they would only let it.

"When he read Walt Whitman, Walt Whitman came alive and spoke to Raymond face to face.

*'O me! So sad, recurring-what good amid these,*
*O me, O life? Answer: That you are here, that life exists, and identity;*
*That the powerful play goes on, and you will contribute a verse.'*

"Raymond sat mesmerized as Mr. Vogel introduced him to other authors that spoke of courage, commitment and unflagging devotion to ideals, passion, morality, opportunity and peace of mind. Victor Hugo's Hunchback became Raymond's alter ego. It was actually quite incredible. How could Mr. Vogel talk about peace and inner strength while all this abuse was being heaped on him?

"Ray was one of the smart ones who saw the message, not the man."

The pastor continued. "I really never got to know Raymond any deeper until he was in his early twenties. He was not suited for the military, and this made him quite depressed. He found it difficult to gain employment and keep it. But he was always reading, and when he engaged in his favorite conversation about his 'heroes,' his eyes lit up and he was transformed to another place. He spoke of the agony and ecstasy of Goethe's Dr. Faustus, who experienced everything that a man could want, but lying on the precipice of Hell, discovered only love of another could save him. "

He grew, not in stature, but in strength of character. It turns out he would need that strength. When he first came timidly into our church, he had been living on the streets almost eight years. He collected cans and washed cars. Anything to eke out an existence.

"On a street corner he frequented was a small hardware store that dealt mainly in paints and painting supplies. It was owned and operated by a man and wife who lived in the upstairs, along with their small daughter. One night Raymond awoke to see the building almost engulfed in flames. Stopping to think was not an option. He told me that he heard the words of Mr. Vogel as he read Walt Whitman's, *Oh Captain, My Captain.*

*'Oh Captain my Captain! Our fearful trip is done,*
*The ship has weathered every rack, the prize we sought is won,*
*The port is near, the bells I hear, the people are exulting,*
*While follow eyes the steady keel, the vessel grim and daring...'*

"The interior of the building was ablaze, but Raymond searched until he found the little girl. He saw the parents but it was too late for them. The fire department came and put the fire out. Raymond gave them the little girl, and he thought that would be the end of it. Besides, what good could he, a homeless bum, do her?

"He watched the papers out of curiosity. The cause of the fire was investigated and was determined to have been caused by an errant electrical spark igniting the volatile chemicals. The child was singed and scared, but otherwise in good shape. Many fine, upstanding people from the community came forward, asking for the right to adopt her. So many, in fact, there would be the need for a court hearing.

"Being a pastor, I get to meet a lot of interesting people. One of the parishioners in our church was Judge William Tallman, who presided over the custody hearings. He filled in the details for me over time. The little girl was lucky. Judge Tallman is a fine man, and in this day and age of moral laxity in our courts, he truly practices justice, tempered with mercy.

"Anyway, the day of the hearing, he told me his courtroom was packed. Raymond was in the back, trying to stay un-noticed in his old clothes and disheveled appearance, but driven by curiosity to see what nice family would be the recipient of this darling little girl. All sorts of people waited in line, hoping to tell the court that they, and only they, were fit to adopt her. Many had brought their own lawyers to prepare papers, should they get the go ahead. What a circus it must have been.

"Judge Tallman brought the little girl up to sit on a chair next to his bench. Her little feet were dangling off the chair. My God, she was a charmer. Little black shoes and a yellow dress. About fifteen people had applied for guardianship. Each one was of good character, well-to-do. They all could have offered her so much. But all through the proceedings the little girl seemed so disinterested. Occasionally she would look up at someone and then look back down at her feet. The judge told me he tried to see if she would respond to any particular person, but no dice.

"After the last candidate came forward, Judge Tallman asked the little girl if she had any preference as to whom she would like to consider as a new mommy or daddy. She sighed and looked all about the courtroom.

"Then all of the sudden her eyes got real wide, she got really excited and jumped off the chair and ran over to a man. Until then, I don't think anyone noticed that Raymond was even there. The judge told me he hadn't either, but it was rather odd. In a courtroom full of noise, he remembered hearing someone coughing and having a difficult time controlling it.

"Anyway, she grabbed at this guy's arm and tugged and tugged, trying to get him to come forward. When he finally stood up, she said 'I want him to be my daddy!'

"Well, talk about disorder in the court! After an uneasy silence was restored, Judge Tallman looked at her (and later told me he will always regret what he said next) 'Little girl. All these fine people want to take you home. Why would you pick him?'

"She looked up at him and you could hear a pin drop. 'Because he saved me!'

"The judge could add nothing further. The crowd began to murmur amongst themselves, and everyone strained to get a better look.

"Raymond became an instant celebrity. But he had no physical address and couldn't have kept the little girl even if he wanted to. One of the applicants was a beautiful young lady and she was allowed to adopt her. After Raymond reluctantly told his story, the media, (being the media), blew it out of proportion, which was exactly what he knew would happen and exactly what he didn't want. But good came from it. He became a moral icon that everyone wanted to identify with, to have a part of. Everyone loves a hero and will not tolerate a loser."

The city set him up in a small apartment. They offered him a furnished townhouse, but he refused. He insisted on a job, and the offers flooded in. The young lady permitted him to visit the little girl as often as he would like. She was scared at first, but he proved to be everything the media painted him to be. He was kind, gentle and sincere. The little girl adored him without reservation. Over time, the young lady fell in love with him too. She figured (wrongly), after the news died down the two of them would have no more use for each other.

"We 'allowed' ourselves to fall in love and we married," she told me.

"I married them in the church. It was a very quiet ceremony, only two or three witnesses. The town would not leave them alone. They could identify with Raymond. Here was an example of strength that grew out of adversity. Here too, was an example of Beauty and the Beast. Raymond, plain and homely, the girl on his arm stunningly beautiful. When the common man thought about how insurmountable his problems were, he thought about Raymond, and then decided his lot wasn't so bad after all.

"They both had their secrets. The young woman's father had invented a certain pickling brine and she became heiress to a good-sized fortune. She never told Raymond. She was afraid he would be like all the rest of a long line of suitors who were looking for a handout. She need not have worried. He was the kind of man who was content with people, not with things. As well off as they were, he always worked.

"In time, Raymond's secrets would surface as well. The cough he could never get rid of was due to the caustic chemicals he breathed the night of the fire. He had seen a doctor and had told no one. The prognosis was not good. He told his young bride as he was dying that he almost left her before they were married because he didn't want the little girl to lose another father.

"A few days before he died, he was in and out of consciousness, but had a moment where he was just lucid enough to ask to see three people. Me, his daughter, and Mr. Vogel. I didn't have the heart to tell him Clarence Vogel had died a few years earlier."

I had long since stopped thumbing through the papers and had become a rapt listener. I would give my full attention to the deceased and send him off as befit a hero. A hero of the common man.

I remember this case. Raymond Mason was lying on the table allowing me to ply all the skills of my trade to him. I dressed him as befitted a king. I took a step back to survey a truly wonderful transformation. Suddenly it hit me yet again. I could almost imagine him crying out *I am not a hero. This is not me. Get rid of the suit and tie and find me a plain shirt and slacks.*

"But Ray," I protested in our imaginary dialogue. "The Mayor and the City Council chipped in and bought you this beautiful suit."

*Hey, Michael. It's my funeral.*

I remember this case as one that took me a long time to prepare. I remember Mr. Thomas' words and Mrs. Thomas' berating. Like it or not, Raymond Mason was right. It was his funeral and his wife and daughter would not let him go until I got it right.

Raymond's funeral was held a few days later. The mediocre, and those who were down on their luck and were struggling were well represented. In life and in death he would be their champion.

At the funeral, we were finally introduced to the little girl, who had blossomed into a very beautiful and poised teenager. He had given her the only gifts he knew – confidence and morality. At the funeral, she stood and read haltingly, a poem for Raymond she composed herself:

> *"A life, lived short and well*
> *Little time, your beauty to dispel*
> *Now all in Heaven hear the decree!*
> *His crown of righteousness shall be!"*
> *So now dear Father released and free*
> *Glory at last revealed to thee!*

I am sitting at home, many years later, and remember some of the words the mourners spoke in eulogy. The pastor is telling the assembled there are no tears where he is now, but he could imagine Ray watching the proceedings and weeping – with joy.

Several people came up to touch the casket and have one last look inside. The stories I heard were amazing. One youngster looked at him and said 'You broke up a fight between a big bully and a small child. You received a broken collarbone for my troubles, but all I could think of was you and your courage, and you strengthened me. I went on to help develop a new treatment for children affected with cerebral palsy.'

Another older man came and stared. He said, "I was ridiculed for years and could never make any friends. I joined the Navy at sixteen, lying about my age. I received two Purple Hearts, and a Medal of Valor for pulling wounded men away from a fire fight. You were with me then, telling me of the Hunchback laying down his life for what he loved.'

A girl came to touch the casket, frankly, looking worse than Ray did, even with the work we did. She was crying, her tears falling on his face. "You have given me the courage to face my death now. I have terminal cancer and I was pregnant and they wanted to abort my baby. I wouldn't let them. I heard you talking to your little girl about fighting the unpopular fight, against all odds, and against all those telling you to do otherwise. You were my 300 Spartans all in one."

And I could imagine Ray telling me, "Hey, Michael. Do me a favor, will you? Tell those people it wasn't me. It wasn't any courage on my part. Tell them courage only rears its head when you are hungry enough, tired enough, or disgusted enough, to do something. And another thing... If they witness acts of morality, ethical behavior, and love in action, tell the person while they are alive. I know it sounds selfish, but I would have liked to have heard these stories from them personally. At any rate, Michael, be an encourager."

# Chapter 12:
# A Suitable Heart.
# The Story of Louis Felan

Death comes once, for all. Many times we see those grieving who will not, cannot, let go. But the dead remain dead. I saw this several times, but the one that stood out was a man that had a story worth repeating. Only in his own death, perhaps would he unburden his persistent, oppressive grief and experience eternal joy. Perhaps he and the object of his grief could at last be reunited and all their trials would finally be forgotten.

One afternoon we received a decedent from a local hospital. The name band read Louis Felan. His features were non-descript, a man in his late sixties, casually dressed. He had arrived in a hospital emergency room and had succumbed to whatever ailment that had sent him there. None of the usual telltale marks of revival attempts were noticeable. His open shirt revealed traces of cardiogram patches, perhaps slapped on in a desperate attempt to diagnose a lethal problem. Looking at his face I could not help but notice a deep furrow in the skin just underneath both eyes.

Ed introduced me to the wife and a son. All stressed to me that the man had a rose clutched in his hands, and it was absolutely not, under any circumstances, to be disturbed. I was to prep him for a casket burial.

The mortician as a makeup artist strives to make the deceased appear as they were known. We take a father, dead from cancer and emaciated from the disease, and by filling out his cheeks and coloring his features just so, have it appear that he was actually a bit heavier. But as I found out with Mr. Thomas, too much of a good thing will destroy the character and erase potent history.

Yet, death must imitate art, and many a surviving relative has asked us to recreate the corpse as they remembered him or her during a defining moment. I remember the family of a judge wishing that he look stern and imposing. The mother of a junkie and prostitute wanted us to recreate her little girl's innocence. A twenty-year-old picture accompanied a ninety-year-old woman. Could we turn back time accordingly? Mourners want to love, forgive, trade fond stories and cry.

All bodies, including Mr. Felan's, bore a history. In school, I became adept at reading the story, but Ed taught me how to appreciate it. This man had a tattoo with the wife's name. Clean shaven, even in death. A scar from an appendectomy. No hair on his ankles. Receding hairline. The hand clutched the rose. Were there thorns? I didn't dare to look. All marks were clues to the man's character and how he lived. I have buried a lot of dead. I wonder, what would the funeral director see, looking down on me when my time came?

Initially, my task with Mr. Louis Felan seemed easy. Never allow the rose to leave his hands and use makeup that accentuates the tracks under his eyes. The more I listened to Mr. Felan's story, the more intensely human he became, and the more difficult my job. The family requested his final repose to convey deep, everlasting sorrow.

The handsome young man that accompanied Mr. Felan's widow was one son. There existed somewhere another surviving son, and a few years earlier, a daughter who had died in a traffic accident. The story of Mr. Felan was not about Mr. Felan, but of the daughter. Through tears, they filled me in as we sat at the conference table completing the obituary.

The wife began. "We had a daughter named Natalie. She was by no means a perfect little girl, but she was definitely Daddy's little girl. As kids are apt to do, she would bring home crafts made at school addressed to Daddy, a hand print made of clay, a tiny heart with his and her names on it... stuff like that. He would smile and place them tenderly in a keepsake box we had in our bedroom.

"Don't get me wrong. We loved all our children so much, and their father was a wonderful role model. He allowed the children to get into trouble to the point where they would cry out to him and then he would help them, hoping they would learn from their mistakes.

"The children grew and went their own ways. They all succeeded in their endeavors, and we were so proud of them. Natalie just seemed to learn lessons a little slower than the others. The harder her father tried to discipline, to pass on to her life skills, the more she resisted. She didn't want to face the world. I think she was afraid. Both dad and daughter knew each other's weaknesses. Whenever she asked for yet another favor, I would say no, and she would seek him out. He would try, truly try, to say 'no,' but in the end he would go to the keepsake box and finger all the little trinkets. He would sigh and invariably give in."

She turned her head in an effort to compose herself. The son stared at his hands in his lap and could only add at this point, "None of us ever got into trouble with the law, and we all got decent grades. We made it a point to see our dad lots of times after we moved out. Even Natalie came, which was sort of surprising. I never could get close to my sister, because I thought she was selfish and lazy. She barely graduated from high school, hung out with the wrong people, got in over her head with traffic tickets and couldn't keep a job. She returned home a lot, and I figured it was because she thought she could talk Dad out of a few bucks, but, she really would come by with no other motive than just to be with him."

He stopped. He had made no effort to hide his bitterness.

The widow continued. "The patterns repeated themselves. She would ask, he would go to the box. Over time, she landed a mediocre job, cultivated decent friendships, and began taking vocational classes at the nearby city college. Things seemed to be going as well as they could for her. I expected more, wanted more, but Louis was content in knowing she was safe and happy. One time I remember seeing Louis in our room after she left from a visit. He was fingering the trinkets and looking up at the ceiling and just saying 'thank you,' repeatedly.

"She surprised him one day by showing up on a new bicycle. Initially she had asked him for money to buy a car, and it about broke his heart, because he had to gently refuse. She needed transportation, so she found her own solution. We felt this was a huge turning point for all three of us. She had a need, and she found her own solution with no help from Louis. Then one night, we were both dozing in our easy chairs catching only snippets of the evening news on the TV. Somehow, we both managed to hear '…earlier this evening…a nineteen-year-old girl, riding a bicycle …struck in a crosswalk…'"

At this point the mother covered her mouth with her hands and ran out of the room, sobbing. The son moved to overtake her, but I touched his shoulder and motioned him back to his chair. "Leave her alone with her memories," I said. "She will return in her own time."

The son slowly sat down, looked about somewhat nervously, and continued. "Dad told us he awoke and put his face real close to the TV, thinking there was just no way it could be Natalie.

"But the call would come. She had been identified by the cards in her purse. The hospital told them they needed to come quickly. Mom and Dad called me and we all met there. They told me on the phone that it did not look good.

"We got there and we waited. Then we were taken into a room. Soon a doctor, a nurse and a policeman came in. The policeman told us he was on routine patrol when he saw traffic slowing, and someone ran to his window and shouted that there had been an accident up ahead. It was Natalie."

The son was finding it difficult to continue. His legs were crossed and he moved the top leg up and down rapidly as he bit his lip. How long he fidgeted and how long I sat in silence was anyone's guess. The door opened and Ed and the widow entered, Ed with his arm around her. They both sat down. The wife touched the boy on the arm, and he said, "I was telling him about going to the hospital and talking with the policeman."

The mother became animated. "Did you tell him what she was carrying? She was carrying a box of cookies with pink frosting fresh from the bakery. Those were my husband's favorite.

"Natalie died doing a selfless act for her father. Anyway," she continued, "after the policeman left, the doctor just looked at us for a bit and told us he was going to run some tests and that it didn't look good."

She spoke the last few sentences rapidly, then she looked about her, eyes darting. She slumped into her chair and talked, slowly now, her voice soft. "It was obvious that the doctor was very uncomfortable. He stood up and almost headed out the door as he was talking. He said something like, 'We're going to run some tests, but all her vital neurological signs are absent. It doesn't look good.' Then he sped off.

"The nurse remained. She sat there, allowing us to absorb all we had been told those first, brutal moments. Then she simply said, 'She was your daughter. You need to think about making the toughest decision you'll ever be faced with. If things don't turn out well, would you be able to find it within yourselves to consider donating her organs to others?'

"My husband hadn't said much since we arrived, but at this he completely broke down. 'Do you hear what they are saying?' he said. 'They are speaking of her in the past already. She was my daughter. I was her father.'"

I sat back, lost in my own thoughts. I knew where the story was heading. The family must not have had any idea of the importance in the part they would play. Certainly their battered daughter did not. Natalie was a nineteen-year-old girl in perfect health except that she would never see, hear, touch and laugh again. Now they must confront and witness her death.

The wife continued. "I remember the nurse saying, 'I am sad for you because your daughter is dying. There is nothing we can do for her. You want her to live, we want her to live, but she cannot. However, there is another person who can live with her heart. There are two others who can live with her kidneys. There is a person who will no longer need insulin shots because they can live with your daughter's pancreas. A blind child will see because of her corneas.'

"Most people would not agree, but our daughter gave my husband so much, and it didn't take him long to make the decision to donate her organs. Better to keep on giving than to destroy a heart in a pile of ashes."

She stayed seated, but what we read in her eyes let us know she was far away.

The son spoke again. "I was with my father as he cradled her head in his hands and spoke about her to the nurses, orderlies, anyone who would listen. We kept a vigil at her bedside. The beeps of the machines, the rise of her chest, the warmth of her face, all that told us she was alive, but our own minds told us otherwise. Finally, they came in and told us it was time for Natalie to go. All the testing was complete. There was no more stalling for time. We must let her go now. She had been declared brain dead by doctors of varying specialties who could be objective because they had no interest in the case, professionally. Dad asked for, and was granted, a last few minutes alone with her. Alone, with her and his thoughts."

"He was not strong enough to witness her being rolled down the corridors, still warm, pink, willingly being pushed to her doom. He had been crying almost non-stop since he had entered the hospital. He left the room and walked the other way as the orderlies came in and wheeled her away. After they took her, he walked the corridors. He returned to the room. Maybe it had all been a mistake. Maybe his angel would be there, smiling.

"He caught up with my mother and me in the waiting area. A white rose was pinned to his jacket. He told us that when he returned to her empty room, he had found the rose that some anonymous person had left in a vase with her name on it."

It was here that I got up and left the room. The grief was oppressive. Ed would sit with them awhile longer. I went to the cooler and retrieved the father. I looked down and spoke to him and assured him that I had not left the conference room early. I knew the rest of the story.

Natalie, her skull cracked, cognizance destroyed forever, would never again focus on anything, even this last kind act of a stranger who left her the white rose. No more whispers, no more laughs, plenty more tears. All because the pieces were falling apart. So, my friend, what else could you do but give the pieces away before they died? It was a gesture worthy of a great exit. The heart was worthy of the transplant.

I found out from Ed later that the father took the rose and put it in the keepsake box until time for her funeral. It was his symbol of hope for the living. It would be the first of many that would be sprinkled on her grave. After her funeral he would wear a white rose, until it was time for his own funeral.

Louis Felan died a few years after his daughter. He cried almost daily. The two deep marks under his eyes were the tracks made by tears. The rose left by the unforeseen Good Samaritan was, indeed, the first of many to be placed on her casket. Leaving the gravesite, the father plucked another rose to put in the keepsake box. During his remaining years, as one rose wilted it was replaced by another. When he stared at the rose and his thoughts drifted, he would not cry. The rose represented hope that his daughter had given others. It must never leave his hands. It must be buried with him. Because, you see, hope dies last.

*Hey Michael... do you know who this is? Do you know that I have a keepsake box for you? I'm just waiting for you to ask a favor of me so I can go to the box and look at the trinkets that represent your life; represent our relationship, so that I can give you what you wish. But there is a catch... you gotta ask.*

# Chapter 13:
# To Sir, From Irma, With Love

Carson's Funeral Home was beginning to make me uncomfortable. After five years I still loved my job but at times I hated what it was doing to me. The person who always relied on his own strength, never needing anybody, was melting away, albeit somewhat slower than the drenched witch from The Wizard of Oz. It was taking a long time for the old Michael to rest in peace, as it were, and accept the new Michael that was fighting to be heard.

I found myself seeking out co-workers to bounce questions and ideas off of. I was no longer so much of a loner.

One very embarrassing encounter I remember was being asked by a co-worker if I would like to go out with the crew after hours to grab a bite. I asked him for his name and how long he had worked there. He told me he had been employed at Carson's before I arrived.

I asked where he worked, as I had not noticed him.

"Friend," he answered, "I have been here all along. Where have you been?

Priorities: All of us have them. The smart people change them often, realizing that so much of life, many of our thoughts, many of our possessions, are fleeting.

The way we think: Often it is a sad testimony of man's fascination with the "now."

Not so with Irma Glendale. She was a friend I met who got it right, but Irma paid her dues. Some well-meaning person introduced her to her husband Roger, and their marriage lasted many, many years.

Hey, Irma! You, in turn, did a good deed. You introduced me to my wife Adelina and we were married for 50 years.

The late Irma Glendale came to Carson's, as one of the innumerable, faceless little old ladies. The name "Glendale" sounded familiar. I rummaged through the files and there it was. Carson's had cremated her husband Roger sometime back. He was seventy-nine when he died. She was eighty-two. He lived in a nursing home the last eighteen months of his life, his mind obliterated by Alzheimer's. She died in a beautiful home, and she remained spry and lucid to the end.

In reviewing the records and speaking with the nursing home staff that knew the Glendales, I found nothing out of the ordinary. However, the mere fact that they had been together fifty years prompted me to dig a bit further. I took a chance that somewhere in the lives of these two perhaps a lesson might be uncovered. Was Roger's death from Alzheimer's purely bad genetics? I remember reading studies that have shown time and time again that in long-term marriages, both people have a better chance of avoiding some of the pitfalls of the aged; memory loss, depression, whatever.

I am visiting the mausoleum, in front of the niche where Adelina's remains rest. "Hey, beautiful," I whisper. "Perhaps we made it after all. You never gave up. I may lose my senses, I may lose everything I own, but I will always keep the memories of you. Have you met the Glendales yet? Is their story as close to you as it is to me? After all, they did introduce us!"

In my quest to see if there was something to be learned from the Glendales, I contacted the nursing home where Roger had lived for the last years of his life. The staff invited me to come to see them, because they were eager to tell the Glendales' story in their own words.

I showed up at the appointed day and time to a nursing home that was not what I expected. There were no revolting smells. The carpets were clean. The rooms were well lit. I know, sadly, that this is what money can buy, and it is not the norm.

I was shown into a room furnished with tables, chairs, a refrigerator and microwave. The young girl who accompanied me told me it was the staff lounge and the nurses who would be meeting with me would be along in a bit. I accepted her offer of a cup of coffee.

Somewhere through the walls I could hear a radio, tuned to a classical music station. There was a solo piano melody. I mean, it had to be a radio. The music was superb. I assumed because of the opulent surroundings that the music was being piped in through speakers placed throughout the facility.

It was not all idyllic; the coffee was horrible, and there was not enough cream or sugar available to salvage the taste.

I thought about asking someone to turn down the music, but then again, this was not my home and the music was beautiful.

Finally, a dark-haired woman entered and introduced herself as Adelina, the charge nurse. I went to take her hand, and I recoiled. She was quite beautiful, and my unease must have shown. I judged her to be about five years my senior.

She gave me a quizzical look and I sat down, flustered.

"My name is Michael. I work at Carson's Funeral Home. Thank you for inviting me."

She smiled, and I forgot about time and place. She said something like "We have to wait for another worker who wanted to be in on the story…" but I was beyond paying attention.

I forced my mind back to the present and we made small talk with the beautiful piano music in the background.

All too soon the door opened again and a young girl with a name tag that read "Monica" came in and took a seat. She thrust a hand my way while simultaneously taking a drink from a soda.

"Hi. My name is Monica. I was one of the medical assistants who knew Irma and Roger." She was young, full of energy. Her eyes darted back and forth. She was a racehorse waiting for the starting gate to open.

Adelina began the story of Irma and Roger Glendale. "It was fun talking with Irma. She lit up so when she talked about Roger, even with all his faults. Roger was one of the good guys. Personable, reasonably handsome, didn't take himself too seriously. He was one of those fortunate people in that everything he put his hand to came out quite well. He had some college, and then he joined the Navy. He tried many different vocations, and his diverse education served him well in the military, but when World War II ended, he still lacked direction as a civilian. His family had been poor, and he had never had much money.

"He had traveled a lot and seen the best and the worst the world had to offer."

Monica, the attractive aide, blurted laughingly. "Yeah. Then he met Irma, and his life changed overnight."

Adelina nodded. "Irma told this story dozens of times, and each time she got this faraway look and would speak wistfully. At first, she snubbed him, assuming he was just another immature youngster with lofty ideals and neither foot on the ground. He was so young and handsome so sure of himself. She recalls being so angry with him one of the first times she saw him that she never wanted to even see him again. "

It was at a charity dance, and he had the audacity to show up dressed in a tailored naval officer's uniform with rows and rows of campaign ribbons. He had no tact or sense of decency, wearing all those obviously fake medals. It was a slap in the face to all the soldiers who earned them."

Monica rose from her chair and paced as she spoke. "Yeah, but he was a man's man, the kind I want. He saw what he wanted and he went for it. He got 'the disease' immediately, and he got it bad. It's kinda funny. My boyfriend was in Viet Nam, and has seen his share of combat. Roger fought, too, and neither Roger nor my Juan can figure out how to tame one little girl. I can see Roger now. Hovering about, always in her line of sight, and she trying to stay out of his." She laughed the knowing laugh of a woman who can subdue a man with a smile or a well-placed word.

Adelina, being somewhat older and wiser, allowed Monica to tell her side of the story, focusing on what she thought was important. As Monica talked, I looked at Adelina. Could she relate to Monica's youth? They were both so focused on Roger Glendale's looks. Adelina was so beautiful. Certainly she has seen more than her share of suitors I thought. Did she seek for something more than the outward appearance?

At this point, I leaned back, content to listen. The girls were full of delight as they recounted this tale. If some of it sounded a bit embellished, I could not be sure, but they were enjoying laying this groundwork. Of that, I could be sure.

Adelina broke into an even wider grin and became quite animated as she continued. Monica held her soda can in both hands, nodding furiously as the story progressed. "Irma was so sure that he was a big fake. Her own father had been in World War I and she knew what it took to earn those medals.

"Roger finally got up the nerve to talk to her, determined to do so no matter what her reaction. She snorted at him, with disdain. Finally, after several attempts she glared at him and said, 'Why are you following me?'

"All he wanted was an introduction and to introduce himself. She countered by telling him she had no use for 'his kind.'

'What kind is that?' he asked

"She gave him a good tongue-lashing. It was not right to make a mockery of those who fought and died by wearing store-bought medals. She told him he had no right to wear them.

"He threw back his head and laughed. He removed his officer's cap and bowed deeply. 'Allow me to introduce myself. Commander Roger Glendale, Retired. European Theatre of Operations, St. Lo and Marne.'

"The shocked look on her face must have been obvious. She managed to stammer, 'You were in France?' He nodded and she fled.

"About an hour later, he felt a tap on his elbow. 'I, uh, dismissed my escort. Do you want to talk?'

"Three months later, they were married. Never was there a couple more suited to each other than Irma and Roger. Even weeks before her death, you could see her eyes light up as she talked. She would visit him, and she would cry and cry. She would tell us that her tears were full of joy, laughter, memories and there just would never be enough tears to hold them all.

"After the war, Roger took many jobs, just to make a living. He was finally hired on by a fledgling aircraft company, and there he found a purpose for his life. He ascended the ranks quickly. The company prospered and he and his new wife enjoyed the lifestyle afforded to a top executive. The marriage produced two daughters and a son."

I rose, excusing myself to call the office. Donna answered, her usual bland-but-professional self, "No need to hurry back."

I returned to my spot, not terribly wrapped up in the story, but enjoying the animation of the two girls as they told it their way.

Adelina sat back in her chair and she measured her words carefully as she picked up where she left off. "Irma told us that Roger was always driven. She always guessed it was because of his youth. He never had much but he vowed he would never lack for any material thing again.

After fifteen, maybe twenty years, she noticed him looking in the mirror often, and then asking himself, 'Is this all there is?'

"Irma understood his wants and needs but was powerless to help. The way she looked at it, her world was filled with more blessings than she could have imagined. She was content. Roger was panicky. He looked at his world, seemingly perfect; full of possessions and loving children, an attentive wife; yet he wanted more. It grew worse as his hair grayed. He dyed it. He joined a gym. First two days a week, then six.

"The old car had to go. The newness of the next car lasted only a year.

"Irma smiled as she watched her man. She indulged him his desires. She loved him unconditionally. She sat with him at night, caressing his hair, his cheek. He provided well. They were retired, had good health, and lived in a comfortable house.

"Roger's panic grew, becoming more consuming. His unspoken motto became 'more and more, bigger and bigger.' Many of his acquisitions never even made it out of their packages. They lost their appeal even before they arrived in the mail. He fantasized about being in a big crowd, the center of attention, people of all ages hanging on his every word.

Adelina's voice itself took on a sense of urgency. It was as if she was recounting the story in real time. Her eyes widened. She spoke rapidly.

"Irma loved him as he was. He was a caged lion, but he was her caged lion. She cried out to him, 'Roger! We don't need all this. Slow down so you can enjoy all the things you worked all your life to obtain!'"

"A few weeks before he ceased to be the Roger that Irma married, he woke up suddenly in the dark. So sudden that it woke her. He blinked at her and said, 'I had a dream. There was a raven; his death wings outstretched, his caw like an invitation. I was chained to it and I kept crying 'Put me down! Put me down!' And the chains kept getting tighter and the raven kept its slow flight and I knew I would die and I was glad.

"'Yet even as I was being encircled by the chains I felt as if I was circling free. And I looked down and I saw the chains and they weren't encircling me at all, they were held in my hands and I was clutching them in a death grip. To become free and save myself all I had to do was let go. Let go of the chains that were encircling me and float freely. I was a slave and I could be free – all I had to do was to let go.'

"Irma said she took his head in her hands and held him tight. She was grateful. Like a fever, perhaps, his passion for 'things' would break. She whispered incessantly, Let go Baby, let go!

"But it was not to be. He was beyond listening. The more he coveted, the more he hated. Company no longer came to the house. Roger became more and more incoherent. Fearing for their mother's safety from his neglect, his children convinced her to put him here. She sold much of his personal goods that had never even been used, to pay his bills."

Monica leaned over and whispered with conviction, "The diagnosis was Alzheimer's, and even on the death certificate the cause of death was listed as Dementia secondary to Alzheimer's, but everyone here knew better. Irma visited, but soon she became unrecognizable to him. His eyes were always open and searching for something; what, only he knew. His mind was racing in all directions at once. He finally died, empty."

*Eyes open... searching wildly in vain.* I thought of Paul Anderson, The Howling Man.

Monica sat down. Her soda can was drained and in her passion for telling her part of the story, it seemed she was too.

Adelina shook her head almost in pity. "While he was alive he never knew he had two grandsons. Irma brought him and us flowers from the house. He never smelled the night- blooming jasmine in his own front yard. He would never be able to tell the difference between the gentle touch of his wife and the stern grasp of an orderly guiding him back to his room.

He replaced savoring the taste of Irma's fine delicacies with the spoon feeding of mush.

"Irma mourned. Her children moved away. The grandkids visited. She was comforted in front of a warm, inviting fire. The very walls of her house knew they were protecting a lover.

"She lost her world when her Roger died, but she never lost sight of her values and that is what kept her strong and secure. We have a home health program and we cared for her at her house. She died in her own bed surrounded by the things and the people she loved."

I thanked the staff for their time and a most insightful view of a life. I bought Monica and Adelina lunch, promising to keep in touch. The piano music was still playing, still surreal. I arose to leave, but stopped, hand on the doorknob. Adelina sensed my question and she laughed.

"Let me guess. You're wondering where the music is coming from." I smiled and nodded.

"That's Hal Christensen. He used to be a professional pianist. He is a resident here. He still gives concerts and he still draws a fair sized crowd. Come back to hear him play sometime?"

Her invitation might have been a request for a pleasant night of quality entertainment for the both of us. At the time, I was still too interested only in myself to pick up the signal. Besides, her presence shook me and left me unable to think clearly. I mumbled something and left, my only thought being the music, coming from a living being a few feet away.

I remember Irma, because I was sitting at home one night looking over the city. I saw the lights. Some moved, some flashed and some glowed bright, others dull. Was it true? Did Irma learn what Roger refused to? Is it better to live a short life of contentment or a long life of reaching for the unreachable?

In life, Irma listened and found peace and a deep sense of well-being. Adelina, I would find out later, left a lucrative job at a large city hospital and was at peace working with people that time and the twenty-first century had discarded, gladly accepting the poor wages for the joy of being touched by beautiful lives.

I was watching the lights and many had their own story they were preparing... just for me.

At this point in my life I was "hearing" but still not ready to listen. My road to contentment existed; but it was not very well lit. It was not straight and nicely paved, but the names were readily marked. The street signs read "Failure." An on-ramp warned "Confusion." A straight and pleasant-looking stretch signaled with a flashing red light, "Enemies at the Gate." Then I saw the sign beyond. "Loneliness, unfulfillment, despair. I stumbled, but out of the corner of an eye, I thought I saw a sign labeled "Friends."

Years later, those lights and the road signs would change, even for me. The little moving dots became the drivers navigating these roads. They all reached their goal, even though there may have been pit stops along the way. The lights changed. I know well the names of the drivers behind the wheel: Determination. Perseverance. Faith.

No doubt, Irma knew them too.

# Chapter 14:

# No More Piano in the House

I was – maybe still am – guilty of wearing many masks. I would wake up at times and look in the mirror and ask myself, "'Who am I going to be today? The gruff cynic? The sympathetic listener? Sullen? Angry?"

I met Adelina, my wife, through a stranger. Then another lady taught me the value of being myself. I am so thankful she did, because I promised Adelina she would marry the man she was expecting to get, not a chameleon. It was a good thing, too. She held me to that promise, and with the help of the Lady of the Masks, it was a promise that was not too difficult to keep, even though I had relapses at times.

But first, I must tell you of my life-long friend in death, Hal Christensen. The love that would start with the Glendales would be completed by Hal. These people gave me a gift I can never begin to pay back.

It was almost nine o'clock on yet another nondescript day at work. The small box by the phone that served as an intercom came alive with static and I heard Donnas' voice. "Michael, could you please come to the office for a phone call?"

There was a sense of urgency in her usually bland voice so I dropped what I was doing (literally), and headed for the office. Donna held the phone, with her hand over the mouthpiece.

"It's for you," she whispered loudly. "It sounds like a young lady." She emphasized the word "lady," tantalizingly, wanting to be let in on a secret, if there was one.

I took the phone and uttered a hesitant, "Hello?"

"Is this Michael?" The voice on the phone was that of a teary woman. "Yes?" I responded, somewhat like a swimmer testing cold water with a toe.

"This is Adelina, from the nursing home. Oh, Michael, I have some terrible news. Hal Christensen died this morning."

Hal Christensen… Hal Christensen… where had I heard that name before? Then I remembered. I had heard the almost unearthly tunes that Hal had played on the piano at the nursing home while listening to the tale of Roger and Irma Glendale. And, though it had been months, it hit me like it was yesterday: the beauty of Adelina, the nurse in attendance.

All I could say was something banal like, "I am so sorry. What can I do to help?"

These words sound so lofty, so majestic, when speaking with a family in mourning, but now that it was personal, to me they sounded trite and hollow.

Adelina was talking through sobs. "I don't know. I just needed someone to talk to. I couldn't think of anyone. You seemed to enjoy him so much. I'm so sorry for crying. He meant a lot to me. I don't want just anyone taking care of him."

I chose my words carefully, not so much for Hal's sake, but for my own selfish interests... to keep her on the phone, to feel the lift just hearing her voice gave me.

"Please forgive me for asking some questions, but I have to. Did he leave any special requests? Does he have family? If he does come here, I will be happy to give him my personal best, but that is not my call."

Adelina was obviously not thinking clearly, and all she could say was, "I'll call you back as soon as I find out some more information. If I need to, can I call you again, just to talk?"

"Absolutely. Anytime. I would be upset if you didn't"... words with an ulterior motive.

She said simply, "Okay," then hung up.

I tried to shuffle out the door, head down, thinking, but Donna was looking up at me expectantly, awaiting an explanation.

I sighed. "I met a nurse a while back who works at a nursing home here in town. A patient she was very fond of died and she wants to make sure he will be treated with dignity and respect."

Donna shook her head as if satisfied with the explanation and returned her gaze to her desk. I wandered back to my desk in the preparation room to catch up on paperwork. I found it almost impossible to concentrate, and as the work load was light, I convinced myself to leave early.

The following evening, just before closing, Ed cornered me in the prep room.

"It seems like you have a fan," he started. He knew, and he knew that I knew what he knew.

Ed continued, that grin still on his face. "I received a call from a nursing home. They have a potential client for us, but they only want you to handle it."

At first I had no idea what he was talking about, and why I would be afforded such a courtesy. Then it hit me. I was flustered when it struck me what Ed was referring to. "I'm sorry," I stammered, "I didn't mean to..."

Ed raised his hand and cut me off. He chuckled. "I'm just tickled for you. If you work anywhere long enough, no matter what your line of work, you are bound to acquire a following. You should be pleased. Apparently, there is someone who sees something in you that you can't, or won't, see in yourself. Everyone here has had clients that have requested them personally. We don't have your person yet, but I'll let you know if he comes our way."

As he was leaving, he turned around, still smiling. "Sounds like you have a very nice young lady in your corner." Before I could reply, he was gone.

Hal Christensen arrived later that night, dressed in a turtleneck shirt and casual slacks. When I arrived for work the following day, I noticed a note pinned to the man's shirt: "Please cremate him with his shirt on."

"Sure," I thought. "Why not? I have had stranger requests." Hal could wait for a day or two. There was to be no viewing and the signed death certificate would be here by the following day.

Later that day, Ed called me into the office and waved a letter at me that had arrived from the nursing home where Hal had been a resident. I unfolded it and saw flowery handwriting. "Hal Christensen has an interesting story. He was a man admired by literally, millions. Give me a call if you're interested." It was signed "Adelina."

I couldn't get to a phone fast enough. I dialed the nursing home listed on Hal's information sheet.

After being transferred and placed on hold by several people, I finally heard Adelina's voice.

"Hi," she said in a subdued voice... not in tears this time. "You're calling about Hal?"

"I must admit, your note intrigued me. Would you like to get together?"

"Yes. When and where?"

"Should I come out there?" I asked.

She sounded mildly disappointed. "Can't we make it somewhere else?" She succeeded in gaining my full attention.

"Uhm...Okay. Any suggestions?"

She perked up a bit. "There is a small restaurant a few blocks from here. Very rustic, very small. It's called Frogmore's. The food is superb. I really like it, but I can't get anybody to take me. Meet me there and I promise you a fascinating story."

She couldn't get anyone to take her there? Unlikely, given her looks. My spirits sank. Was there a glaring flaw, physical or otherwise, in this lady that was about to be revealed? She was almost certainly going to end up being very prim, proper, correct, and all business. Maybe that was it. I thought for a moment before answering. "Well, Okay."

We agreed to meet the following evening for dinner. As soon as she hung up the phone, I became nervous and unsure of myself, regretting I had made arrangements to see her, especially outside a work environment. I would have preferred the conference room where at least I had the familiarity and control of my environment, but I feared the conversation would take too long to try to squeeze in during working hours and we would be interrupted.

I fretted about the next day, looking at my watch all too often. What face would I wear? What persona would I assume? Even though this wasn't a date, I knew myself well enough to know I was not much of a conversationalist, and in reality, functioned just fine as a loner. But on the other hand, Adelina's beauty alone was a reason to see her again. She carried herself with poise, yet confidence. I could sense that this beauty had depth and that is what scared me, but at the same time made me curious. Would she respond better to a firm voice? Confidence? Or should I approach her casually, letting her guide the conversation and make all the decisions? I just knew that being myself would only make her turn away. But wasn't that what I wanted anyway?

I left work early after assuring myself I wasn't taking any lingering smells of my profession with me. I found the restaurant without difficulty, but I couldn't believe my eyes. Frogmore's was just as Adelina had described it. The parking lot was large enough for, perhaps, ten cars. From the outside, I guessed it might be able to seat twenty-five people, tops. The wooden siding of the building was white and in disrepair. There were three picnic tables set on a lawn checkered with brown dead patches.

I thought, *This is the taste in food you have? This is where you want to spend an evening?*

I remained in my car, awaiting her arrival. It wasn't long until I noticed a mid-size white car pull into the lot, and she stepped out. She was still in her work clothes, and for that I was grateful. The more casual the encounter, the better. I took a moment to size her up, to look at her as if for the first time – clinically, objectively. Dark hair, not dyed. Possible Central American heritage? Could use a little more makeup. A few years older than I. Probably never had a child. Fit, with graceful movements, but a physique not sculpted in a gym.

I came up beside her as she was closing her car door. She turned at my approach, gave a little smile and stuck out her hand.

"Thank you for indulging me," she said.

I took her hand in return, enjoying the sensation.

The tables inside Frogmore's were wooden, covered by easy-to-clean tablecloths. There was a sign near the cash register that read "Seat Yourself." No big surprise there, I thought. There was an empty booth in a corner with a wooden seat and padded back. We headed to it and sat down. She looked up at me and casually remarked, "So much to tell you; I don't know where to begin. How was your day?"

I looked down at my hands and shrugged. "So-so, I guess."

Almost as a scold, she shook her finger at me. "Now look here, Michael, I have an intriguing story to tell, but you have to be an animated part of this conversation also."

I leaned back and smiled, all my assumptions how I would take control of this meeting evaporating. She was pleasantly assertive, and would not be easily manipulated.

"All right. I'll do my best. Work was fine, I kept busy... you know, I just don't know how to describe the job I do and leave out the details. Suffice it to say that I like it and it holds enough interest for me to last a lifetime."

I was saved from reaching for further small talk by a waitress who materialized out of nowhere, looking like about what I would expect to find here. Fifty-something, hair damaged from too much coloring, lots of makeup that was not doing its job. "Can I get you folks something to drink to start?" she said as she slid menus towards us.

"Iced tea, please," I said, then caught myself. Should I have let her order first?

*Oh for cryin' out loud,* I thought. *Am I going to second guess myself the whole evening?*

"Make that two," added Adelina. If there was a faux pas, she did not let on.

After the waitress left, she looked at the menu, less preoccupied than she had seemed earlier. "This is such a treat for me. I imagine in your profession you have had ample opportunity to realize that outward appearances aren't always what is reflected on the inside.

Somewhere, perhaps, I heard a voice. It was Dan, the Biker. "Hey hey, Buddy! Don't be too quick to judge a book by its cover! You'd be surprised at the people who made it here. Many of them would not be here if they had to meet your standards."

Her voice brought me back. Had she noticed I had left her for a few seconds? "Choose anything on the menu. I guarantee you won't be disappointed."

I looked at the menu. Most of the dishes were literally, on the menu. I played it safe and waited until Adelina decided.

She pointed to my menu and said, "Try the Beef Stroganoff. Quite good."

I closed the menu, grateful she had decided for me, but when the waitress came with our tea and to take the order, Adelina asked for the fettuccini. When I looked at her somewhat quizzically, she said, "I had the Stroganoff last time. Don't worry, it is really good."

Last time? You told me there was no one to take you here. Just what is your secret? I know a secret can be a barrier to keep the wolfish world at bay, but lady, you lose something lost in its embrace. So tell me now. If there is someone else I am going to be so angry, so disappointed... No wait! This is not a date.

I sipped the tea. Not bad, I thought, but how much talent does it take to brew tea?

Adelina took a deep breath and toyed with her silverware. "Now on to the story of Hal Christensen. Oh, before I forget, when do you think he will be cremated?"

"Probably late tomorrow," I answered, "We will probably have the death certificate signed by then."

She nodded. "I would like to come by before you do, as a friend of the deceased, because I need to show you something."

I shrugged. "Okay. He'll keep."

Adelina looked at me almost in horror. "Michael! I asked for you because I wanted him treated with dignity. Don't you dare become flippant with me!"

I was shocked at the sudden change in her demeanor. I back-pedaled furiously.

"Please forgive me. He is being handled with the utmost respect. I wasn't flippant; it was just a knee-jerk statement. I don't get to talk to many lay people about the things that go on in a job that, unfortunately, has some gallows humor at times. I won't make that mistake around you again."

She seemed satisfied with the response. She crossed her arms, elbows on the table leaning close, and began.

"Hal Christensen had been a famous, wealthy man. He outlived his family, wealth and fame. He died virtually unknown.

"Did you know there is a book written about him? I read it; no, skimmed it, actually. He lived with us for about a year or so, and I got to know him well, outside his book."

At that moment, the waitress returned with bread and salad. She also deposited what looked like some sort of carafe with three individual bowls. She took a pencil from a pocket and pointed.

"These are your salad dressings. This is cranberry vinaigrette. This is Roquefort and cucumber. This one is yogurt and sour cream."

Adelina explained. "All the bread and side dishes here are made from scratch."

I was impressed, but not about to take chances. Funny, I had eaten every imaginable creation in my travels, but I approached this meal with caution. I gingerly poured a spoonful of cranberry dressing on my salad and picked up my fork, picking at it much like I would make my way through a field filled with land mines when Adelina put her hand over mine.

"I don't know where you are from, but it is customary to pray before we eat."

I was terrified. "Pray?" I stammered. "In public?"

So that was it! That was the big secret! I was having dinner with a nun! Where did that leave me? Was the rest of the evening to be bland, listening to her story, then extricating myself as quickly and delicately as possible? Should I play the hypocrite, and if so, for what gain? Would she see right through me? This evening was rapidly disintegrating into rubble and there seemed little chance (or desire), of seeing her after this night.

Adelina pretended to be exasperated. "It's not difficult if you practice. Here. I'll do it this one time, but if we ever do this again, be prepared, Buster!"

We both bowed our heads for what seemed like an eternity. I tried to sneak a glance to see if anyone was watching. Not soon enough, she was through.

Adelina looked at me disapprovingly. "Practice. Talk to Him often. In your car, at work. The more you do it, the more comfortable you two will be around each other."

*Oh great*! I thought. *Beautiful beyond measure but too holy for me. I think we're done here.*

"Anyway," she continued, "back to Hal. Hal was a nice kid, your average all-American boy. He would not have stood out in a playground full of boys. He liked sports, got into boyish mischief, but nothing more than a misplaced water balloon or riding his bicycle the wrong way down a sidewalk. He liked music and had his radio playing almost everywhere.

His parents tried to channel that love of music, trying to encourage him to learn an instrument, but he was too busy just growing up.

"He liked to read. He would read a book he enjoyed over and over, until he could quote great parts of it without error.

"Now here is the part where I am going to start weaving a mystery for you. You have to think, since this is the only clue I am going to give you. When Hal was twelve, he missed a few days of school to have some routine surgery. Since the surgery was done in June, he had the entire summer to recuperate. The surgery was a complete success and he recovered quickly. Much to his parents' delight, he expressed a desire to take piano lessons. They paid for the finest teachers and he learned quickly.

"He loved his newly-found talent because it made him popular. Everywhere he went, there was bound to be a piano nearby. He would sit and play and people would stop and listen attentively, which he craved."

103

I stopped toying with my salad long enough to brave a bite. I dipped a cherry tomato into the cranberry dressing, and I was shocked. I interrupted her story, my mouth not quite empty. "Hey! This salad is dam... darned good!"

She appeared not to have noticed the near solecism, but she seemed genuinely pleased.

"I just knew you'd like it. This place doesn't make many dishes, but they are all as exquisite as the bread and salad."

She picked up Hal's story, this time with more passion. Her eyes betrayed her thoughts. She must have truly loved Hal. It was obvious she loved her job and the patients.

She smiled that disarming smile again and continued. "So Hal learned to play the piano, and he was driven to excel. He spent hours in front of the keys. He could read sheet music with no problem, and then one of his teachers gave him a memorization exercise that started as just that, an exercise. But Hal took it many steps further. He set a radio to a music station that played songs with which he was familiar. He learned to play by ear. Soon he learned to accompany and embellish the songs he heard on the radio. Then he would hear a song he was not familiar with, turn the radio off, and try to play it from memory as best he could. Soon, he had committed long, difficult pieces to memory. What he cherished the most was allowing the piano to 'speak' for him.

"He began college, and there was a piano in the student commons. He would sometimes sit for hours playing for the students who were passing through. Half way through his first year, he quit his classes. He was drawing huge crowds with his impromptu performances, so he thought to himself, 'Why not tour and charge for this?'

"So it was. The demand for his talent grew. At his insistence, he was billed as the man who could make the piano speak. Audiences agreed. His performances were not just about a man sitting in front of black and white keys and tinkling them for the benign amusement of his audience; they were, in fact, a well-choreographed act which caught up his listeners. If the song called for a quick, happy tempo, the lights in the hall would be bright and colorful. If the music was somber, the lights dimmed. He could move an entire audience to tears. By the time the night was over, an individual would leave in a sweat, having run the gamut of emotions. All this, and there would be no sheet music on the piano.

"For the audience, it was mesmerizing. For him, it was almost a drug. He was asked to write an autobiography, and he agreed to do so, but never found the time. Nevertheless, many unofficial accounts appeared on the shelves just the same.

"He entertained for years. He toured the world because the language of the piano is universal. It was the same on every continent. Audiences cried, then they cheered.

"He aged and retired, but always found time to give small, private concerts for friends. He never resided in one town long enough to truly call it home, but finally settled here. For the last five years of his life he lived very comfortably in our assisted living community."

She paused and toyed with her tea glass. The waitress returned with the food, warning them the plates were hot. I stared down at my plate. The food actually looked palatable. Adelina did not hesitate, but twirled the pasta expertly and savored her first bite. "Oh, my," she sighed. "What a treat."

I chased a piece of beef and skewered it with my fork. I, too, was delighted with the first bite. The meat was tender and spiced to perfection.

We enjoyed a superb meal, and her conversation became more interesting to me, now that I had nothing else on my mind.

"That's about all I can remember from the book, only highlights really." Then she was silent again.

There was sadness in her eyes, but a faraway twinkle as well. I broke the spell by saying, "So that was who I heard. I sure wish I could have heard more."

She nodded and finished her story. "During the last year of his life he needed more care and was moved to a skilled nursing facility, which had neither skill nor much nursing, for that matter. I am sad to say that because I am a registered nurse and should have known better. I discounted him and others as individuals who had lived their lives and now there was nothing more they could offer anyone. I lumped them all under the heading of little old folks who, I was sure, were content to live out their days playing cards or sniffing flowers or whatever banal things old people do. "

"But now, I am going to spend the rest of my career making it up to him and others like him. Our elderly have given us so much and they have so much to offer. Now it is my turn to give back to them. A job has to have a meaning. I hope you are doing your job because you want to, not because you are forcing yourself to, but I would imagine in your line of work it is a choice, not a drudgery."

I smiled and looked down. "Wisely spoken. I work because I enjoy what I do, and I am good at it. My boss is trying to get me to see the meaning in what I do. Now that's work."

Adelina drummed her fingers on the table and glanced about. "You have a kind face, and I am going to tell you something because I feel you won't use it against me. I was a hospital nurse, and a very good nurse. Coming face to face, day after day, with the weakness of man, the inhumanity of man toward others, the unfairness leveled against me by my bosses who I thought had my best interests at heart, the hypocrisy I had to tolerate, sort of put me into a tail spin. I had a bit of a 'crisis,' shall we say. I left hospital nursing and never returned. Sometimes I think I would like to go back, but then bad memories surface and I realize I can't go back because I am terrified.

"When I took the job at the nursing home, I could not have cared less about the patients there. It was a job, and they stood in the way between me and collecting my pay every two weeks."

She sighed deeply. "Can you imagine having your family in a place such as that, where the patients have no hope, and the staff has no compassion? Anyway, awhile back, I don't know what started it, but I began to really take notice of the people there. I sat with them. I held their hands. "

Physically, we have a very nice facility, but the staff turnover rate is atrocious, and for the most part, they are a bunch of zombies. In an era of portable music, portable T.V, where teachers are not allowed to teach right and wrong, where few people care about anyone but themselves, people like Hal are being cared for by those who could care even less. "

In that entire facility, I think I am the only one who knows Hal's story, or who cared enough to learn about the man. Do you know we have a lady a few doors away from him who holds two Ph.D.s and has written numerous books? Do you know we have a man who was in the Battle of Leyte Gulf and who shot down seven enemy planes?"

She stopped. She looked exhausted. I had a strange feeling all of a sudden, that at this moment in time, this was where I was supposed to be. I had felt guilty earlier because I had entertained ulterior motives, and now I found myself savoring this moment in time more than I could ever have imagined; even though I felt she was indirectly addressing me in my imperfections, my weakness, my hypocrisies, but it was okay. Coming from anyone but her, at a different time or place, her story would have had no impact at all.

"You have a kind face..." Was it me or the face I keep for special occasions?

We both picked at the remainder of our food, silently. I cleared my throat and asked, "I have two questions. First, I take it there is something I am missing in all this about Hal?

"And second, just out of sheer curiosity, how is Monica, the girl I met at your work?"

"Remember? Earlier I told you that I had a mystery and you would need to listen closely to the story? Think about it and I will stop by your work tomorrow. As for Monica, her boyfriend is back home on leave and she is pregnant."

Then, as almost an afterthought she said, "...and he's leaving soon to go overseas again. She sighed sadly. "I feel sorry for her, and she can't understand why I feel sorry for her. Assuming her boyfriend returns to her, it is still difficult to raise a child in this day and age. How can you raise a child to be strong and moral in such a corrupt society that we live in, overlooking the fact that Monica probably will not marry this man? Lying and cheating are the accepted norms and they are embraced, even applauded. Everyone expects something for nothing..."

*Good grief,* I thought. *Enough of the pontificating. Can't you just make small talk like a real human? Sure. I'm young and I would like a girlfriend. I almost chased after this girl. Being with her is about as exciting as watching paint dry. I mean, I want to be moral, but there is time enough for that later. I'm glad I found out about her now. Oh well, another week and we probably won't see each other again.*

I leaned back and rubbed my hands on my knees. I made sure she saw I was smiling.

"I'm almost sorry I asked."

We finished the meal, and I accepted the check. Adelina mentioned that she would be glad to pay her portion, and I responded, "I'll tell you what. You pray, I'll pay."

She could not stifle a grin, but added somewhat seriously, "Don't let that be your guide, or I promise, you will pay."

I paid the bill, leaving a generous tip; somewhat out of character. Whether I was doing it for Adelina's benefit or because the food truly had been superb, I was not sure. We walked to her car, and again she offered her hand. I was glad she made the overture, because I had no clue of what to do, what to say.

She smiled and said, "I'll come by tomorrow, late afternoon. I would like to see Hal one more time. Thank you for the nice dinner." I watched and waited as she drove off, relieved that the dinner was over, feeling ambivalent about needing to see her the following day, but at least it would be all business, on my turf.

First thing the following day, I requested permission from Ed to allow Adelina to witness Hal's cremation. I explained that Hal had no family and Adelina was the closest he had to someone that cared for him. Ed gave his consent readily, and motioned for me to have a seat.

"So," he started. "How has it been going? Before you get too worried, I am asking as a friend. Your work is impeccable. You seem to be getting along now quite a bit better with others than when you first came. I personally have noticed you seem more satisfied. Tell me. Am I all washed up?"

I took a moment to think. "I feel good. I like what I'm doing. I have met a lot of great people, living or otherwise."

Ed assumed his usual relaxed posture, leaning back in his seat with his hands intertwined behind his head. "I've never fired anyone, although you came close after the Thomas case... not for the job you did on him, mind you, but for your response and your attitude. You failed, and you would not admit it. It took you a long time to get over that and I was waiting for the day you would come into the office with your resignation letter. But I'm glad you stuck it out. I would hate to have thought I was wrong about the potential I saw in you.

"I like my employees to think. I like to ask them difficult questions. The relatives and friends of the deceased ask us tough questions all the time, and we have to respond as if we have at least given them some thought. Please. Never feel you have to jump into the same mold I have made for myself. I have my beliefs, and I do what I do for my own reasons. My words to live by will always be 'know what you believe, and why.' Maybe in time you will come up with your own axioms.

"Well, that's it for now, keep up the good work." He turned away, my signal that the conversation was over.

I left Ed's office and headed back to the prep room. I sighed as

I extricated Hal from the cooler and prepared him for the crematory. There was no waste of a life here, the only waste was that in looking at Hal, I thought of Adelina and what might have been. Hal was wearing a black turtleneck shirt, nothing else. I suppressed my curiosity to probe further until Adelina arrived.

I stared at the man's face... a famous man, known by perhaps millions. He was taking a secret with him to the grave that only a few people were aware of, and I would be one of those few, in a couple of hours.

Ed stopped by as I was reviewing the death certificate and preparing to place Hal back in the cooler. "So this is your man. When all is said and done, will you do me the favor of letting me in on his story? Oh, and hey! Can I ask how your lady friend is doing?"

I gave a small, good-natured snort. "She is hardly my lady friend. She makes me nervous. She is trying to make a moral man out of me. Perhaps she will get tired and give up and go away."

Ed shook his head. "No. I see the look in your eye whenever you speak of her. I don't think you will let go that easily."

*This time you're wrong, Ed.*

The workday was coming to a close and I checked the parking lot as four o'clock came and went. It would be no problem to let Hal wait another day, and I was content to go home for a quiet night, but it was not to be. I made one last tour of the parking lot and was just about to head for my own car when I saw Adelina pull in. She bounced out of the driver's seat and ran up to me.

"Hi," she said, a bit winded. "Come on, show me Hal."

We walked slowly to the cooler. I asked her, "Are you going to be okay with all of this?"

She looked up at me. "I think so. Just don't leave me alone with any of your 'friends.'"

We continued walking, and she spoke, a bit of melancholy in her voice.

"You heard Hal play, but only so briefly. You never saw him in his prime. He was a man who brought the piano to life, and for a brief moment in time, people forgot their troubles, forgot their mundane lives. Hal had a penchant for communicating with the individual. He played in front of an audience, but each person knew he was speaking directly to them. No small feat in a nation – no, a world – full of talkers, not listeners."

We arrived at the cooler and I removed Hal. I kept an eye on her. She had beautiful olive-colored skin. A brief hint of color left her face as I wheeled Hal out from among a dozen or so people waiting their turn. He was white and pasty in death, but he seemed at peace. Adelina would not be dissuaded and I admired her strength. She moved close to Hal's side and was not afraid to touch him. I stepped back as she stroked his face one last time and said silent goodbyes. She looked up, and took a second to compose herself.

"Now for the surprise." She hooked a finger in the top of his turtleneck shirt and pulled down the fabric. At almost the same instant she reached to pull down the high neck, it hit me, but I was not about to spoil her moment. The man who spoke to thousands could not speak himself.

Seventy years earlier, the operation Hal had undergone was a total laryngectomy, the removal of his voice box I shook my head slowly in understanding.

"Oh, Michael," she shuddered. "It is all over. It is so tragic. His life is over and I hardly knew him. What now?" She grabbed my arm, almost in a panic.

I enjoyed the sensation of her touch, "My boss says that a life is not cut short, it is just completed." Neither of us moved for a moment. I thought my actions would go unnoticed as I shifted my arm in order to see my watch. The sooner I could get Hal into the crematory, the sooner I could salvage a few hours of time to myself. I proved to be a terrible actor, because Adelina let go of my arm and glared. She took a few steps back. She turned her back to me.

I apologized as best I could for my actions, but even to me it sounded void of feeling. "He is ready to go into the crematory. Since you are listed as family, of sorts, you can witness it if you want. Basically, that just means you watch as I put him in and begin the process."

"How long does it all take?"

"About three hours."

"Then I guess I will say goodbye."

And then the strangest thing happened. Something compelled me to take both her hands, and I asked if I could see her again. Even stranger was her answer.

"No, I don't think so. I get the feeling you are not who you say you are. You're not ready for a relationship and I don't date haphazardly. Perhaps if or when you let down your guard and come out from behind the masks you are wearing, the real Michael can call me. I will know."

Inwardly I was angry, having lost "the game." Outwardly my expression remained passive. Is that what she meant? I breathed a sigh of relief. It was over. No more guessing, no more game playing. She had won but I didn't care.

I accompanied her to her car and watched as she drove away. Far away. Hal was cremated the next day. I knew he was at peace, wherever he was.

*Hey Michael,* he was saying. *I could not speak so I could not be false with my emotions. I could laugh or cry. Anything else, and I had to let the piano do the talking. The piano was my face. Any face I wanted it to be. Inanimate objects can't lie.*

*"You have the luxury of speech. It is a luxury, isn't it?*

# Chapter 15:
# Laura of the Masks

Months passed. Hal and Adelina were gone. I still had not found a girlfriend, even one who would be a nice companion to share like-interests after work. Not that I was actively searching, but I was starting to realize that I was almost thirty and was asking myself if this was all there was to life.

Some of life's worst examples end up being the best teachers. I think of Dan, the biker. One day Ed presented me with a case that taught me the value of honesty, and showed me that a lie can destroy a person.

He called me into the office and gave me a file.

"We don't get many coroner's cases, but we do have to deal with our share of the indigents, and our share of questionable deaths. We have a client at the coroner's office. He will release her after he is finished conducting a psychological autopsy. Some of the people who knew this lady the most will try to help reconstruct the deceased's state of mind prior to her death. The medical examiner will then decide if it is a homicide or not. Should he decide it was suicide, he will release the body to us. "

My interest in this case is purely that, an interest. This lady supposedly suffered from multiple personalities, and she left behind some beautiful masks. We will be tasked with choosing a suitable mask she will wear as she is cremated. I would like your input.

It so happens the M.E. is a friend and he tells me he is leaning toward suicide, and he doesn't mind if you sit in as an observer."

Up to this point in my career, I had been involved with people that had intriguing histories. But a lady of many masks?

The office of the coroner was housed in the police administration building. The property was surrounded by a gate, and once inside, specially coded badges permitted access only to those with business in the specialty areas. The suite of offices belonging to the police forensics department was no exception.

I arrived early. A disembodied voice coming from a speaker mounted underneath a camera asked me to state my business. A gate rattled open.

A secretary escorted me to my destination and instructed me to wait. She was very starched, impersonal, and proper.

The halls were eerie; white, and sterile. The fluorescent lighting overhead was glaring and uninviting.

*Abandon All Hope, Ye Who Enter Here. What layer of Hell is this, Dante?*

Absorbed in my surroundings, I didn't notice a door had opened. Someone cleared her throat and I turned to see a smiling woman with a stenography pad in her hand. I mumbled an apology as she led me to a seat at a table inside a large conference room. There were several others already seated

The man at the head of the table introduced himself. "Hi. I'm Doctor Callaway, the M.E. Why don't we quickly reintroduce ourselves and explain why we're here, then get started."

Since I came in last and took the seat at the opposite end of the table, I was first.

"Michael Alexander, Carson's Funeral Home."

Dr. Callaway broke in. "How's Ed, anyway? Good man. Give him my regards."

I nodded. To his left was the woman who seated me. In front of her sat a machine, probably some sort of dictating device. A logical guess, since one would suspect the meeting would be recorded and printed for posterity. "Gina Locke, secretary," she said.

Next to her was a very attractive woman in her mid-thirties. "Hi. I'm one of the nurses that took care of Laura in the hospital. I was asked to come."

I tried to lock eyes with her, but as she glanced my way there was no interest there. *(Sigh)*

There were four others. They were friends or family members.

Since I had little or nothing to contribute to this, it took very little time for my mind to start to wander. I looked down at the table and noticed a folder with the name "Laura" on it. How or when it got there was anybody's guess.

Dr. Callaway spoke. "We have reconstructed Laura's life as best we could with the help of the people present. If anyone has anything to add, now is the time. Is this a homicide? We will either choose, or not choose, to take further action. If we cannot decide, we will not go forward with this case.

"A few demographics. The decedent's name is Laura Conrad. She was once probably a very attractive lady, about forty at the time of her death; five-foot seven inches, 135 pounds. Significant facial scarring from burns received when she was in her late twenties. She arrived to us from the hospital with six boxes, each containing a facemask. As far as objective data, that's about all I've got."

A man spoke next. Who he was, I didn't remember. The man had introduced himself moments earlier, but I hadn't been paying much attention.

"I was Laura's boyfriend. I thought I was her only boyfriend, but I should have known better. I didn't know much about her from a medical standpoint, but perhaps I can give you some insight to her character.

"I guess Laura was what you might call an 'eight-out-of-ten.' She was attractive, but not stellar. Just about everything she did turned out very well, just not well enough to suit her. She was driven, so an 'eight' in any facet of her life would never be satisfactory. She was an accomplished ballroom dancer, but there were others better. She was beautiful before the accident but there were others more beautiful. She was very intelligent, etc. etc.

"She told me an electrical problem caused a fire in her apartment. She actually walked out of the burning building under her own power. She had vivid memories of waking up in a hospital with bandages covering her face. More vivid still were the looks in the eyes of the nurses as they changed the bandages covering her face. Nothing could hide their shock and sympathy. She told me that they would not give her a mirror, so one night when it was quiet she sneaked into the visitor's bathroom and looked for herself. She was devastated. The only part of her touched by the fire had been her face. I think that was the time it all started to unravel for her…"

The M.E. cleared his throat audibly. He opened a file. "In the interest of time and continuity, let me paraphrase from a report the attending physician dictated for this meeting.

"'Laura underwent multiple attempts at reconstructive surgery for third degree burns to the face. It proved futile for the most part. The red marks faded, but the scar tissue froze her face in a passive, flat smirk. She could not smile. She was referred to a plastic surgeon who supplied her with a lightweight, clear plastic mask so she would not be encumbered with bulky dressings through her recuperation.'"

I remained only mildly interested in the proceedings. Ed was right. I was not going to be able to contribute much. I toyed with the idea of leaving, but my instructions were to be here, and I was sure that Dr. Callaway would tell Ed of my premature departure. Besides, I thought, where would I go? How would I get out of here?

Next was the psychologist. "I became involved with Laura about six months after her accident. Her roommate referred her to me. Laura's plastic surgeon supplied her with six masks at her request. At the time, the roommate was dating a forensic artist who painted the masks with six different faces, almost as a whim, but Laura was thrilled. She bought wigs for each mask. Her confidence soared.

"The roommate approached me in confidence, fearing she had helped to create some sort of a monster. In reality, Laura took on six new personas. In psychologist lingo, I was treating Laura for an obsessive-compulsive disorder. Actually, I was treating all six personalities for basically the same thing. Six entities striving to be the best at whatever they were inclined to pursue.

"It was strange and fascinating at the same time. I learned to recognize who I would be dealing with when she walked through the door, depending on what mask she was wearing. "She picked names for her masks; all beginning with the letter 'L.' The masks were a trigger.

"Laura was a bar hopper, chasing men. Leyna was a magnificent ballroom dancer who became a favorite of the city's dance halls. Leah was shy, a moral alter ego, if you will. Lynette was smart, professional, all business. It was through Lynette that a steady income was possible. She was a self-taught executive secretary.

115

"But Sad Lisa caused her the most trouble. Sad Lisa was always depressed. She was insistent. Life was a dreary act going nowhere. At first, the other personalities chided her for her pessimism, then slowly they began to succumb to the negativity. Laura became tired of sitting on barstools night after night. Lynette wanted a raise.

"The sixth persona, Lucille, helped the real Laura keep a grasp of reality for a time, but the others soon overwhelmed the two sane girls. The girl that was Lynette came out in fewer and fewer sessions. Lucille came in character one session and told me she could no longer control the others. I had no contact with her after that. The barfly was the girl that the real Laura was never supposed to be. She was the lady of the night. She allowed men to buy her drinks and sell her empty promises. If they pressed her, she would excuse herself and slip into another personality, and perhaps go to another bar."

The psychologist finished his story. "Sad Lisa and Laura monopolized her life. Laura almost lost all inhibitions in the bars and a few times she let things go too far and had to run out in fear."

I was only catching snippets of this whole story, because by now I was wondering, *Why aren't we talking to the roommate?*

I heard the last few sentences from the M.E. "This girl was a virgin."

The psychologist nodded. "That would fit exactly with the lifestyle of the six other egos. From what we have been able to piece together about multiple personalities, and it is not an exact science mind you, the central, core character will not allow their alter-persons to be of different moral mindset. As it is in hypnosis, you cannot be coerced into doing something you would not normally do. Would I stake my reputation on it? No. The courts are full of cases of people insisting their alter ego forced them into a life of crime.

"Anyway, the roommate became frightened and told me that when Laura was alone in her room she would talk to the masks, and they would talk back to her, in perfect character. The roommate, by the way, became a patient of mine after she could no longer talk any sense into the real Laura, regardless of which character she was."

*Why would a "sane" person go to a psychologist, just because she couldn't talk sense to someone?* I mused.

"The real Laura had always fancied herself an excellent dancer. It soon became the last vestige of beauty and reality in her life. But one night while dancing, a smiling man looked at her and casually remarked that she seemed to have something weighty on her mind.

She began to cry and snapped, 'What do you want? I'm dancing as fast as I can!'" She ran out.

"That night, the roommate heard her crying well into the early morning hours, and finally it stopped. At first light, she found her on the floor, dead, with a knife in her chest. There was a lot of blood. Even in death she couldn't get it right. She took a while to die. She looked at all the masks, set about on their own chairs, and asked them aloud, 'Which one of you finally convinced her to do it?'"

*Hmm… I thought. Was the roommate crazy like a fox? If she took some time to die, did she cry out in pain? Where was the roommate when all this was happening? Does anybody here really want me to ask any questions?*

The inquest was over. The M.E. asked if there was any input from anyone else, but there was only silence. Slowly, the people around the table gathered their possessions and shuffled out. Dr. Callaway approached me to tell Ed he would contact him with his decision within twenty-four hours. He apologized to me if I thought he had wasted my time.

*Oops.* I thought. *Was I really so transparent that anyone could read me?*

Late that night I stared out at the city lights; the lights on the highway; the lights that Irma Glendale had alluded to in life, and had spoken of to me after her death. One of those lights had just gone out for someone and no one had noticed.

I knew firsthand of facades that people create when reality lets them down. I knew firsthand that those fake characters were fleeting, and would do more harm in the long run, left unchecked.

I heard a girl's voice. *Michael, its Laura. let down your mask! A lie can't last forever, and you will only be attractive to other liars. I should know.*

The following day Ed called me into his office.

"Gordon called... Sorry... Dr. Callaway, that is. He said he is going to pass this case off as a suicide."

"I'm a bit surprised," I interjected. "They should be looking at the roommate. To me it would seem very difficult to stab yourself in the chest. The psychologist there said the roommate is his patient. Perhaps she had this planned and this was part of her attempt to cover her tracks."

"Well, you may be right, who knows? Perhaps there is not enough evidence, perhaps it would cost the city too much to look into it, especially if they were wrong but again, who knows?

"By the way, give Gordon a call, will you? He has something at his office he wants you to pick up, not to mention the deceased. Oh, and a personal favor, please? Give him this with my best regards."

With that, he handed me a box wrapped in plain brown paper.

I phoned the office and identified myself. The operator put the call through. It surprised me she was willing to connect me directly to the ME, and even more surprised that Dr. Callaway picked up.

"Hi. Michael is it?" he asked. "I take it Ed told you we are releasing Laura?"

"Yes."

"Okay. We will have the death certificate ready for you when you get here. Ask for me, will you? I have something you may be interested in seeing."

"Will do, and thanks."

Later that morning I drove to the office and, using the big SUV used to pick up the deceased, backed into the service entrance. Another nameless secretary escorted me to Dr. Callaway's office, and I was relieved that the walls were not so foreboding the second time through. The secretary knocked. The door opened abruptly. It took the M.E. a brief moment, but once he recognized me, he broke out into a wide grin and shoved a meaty hand my way.

"Welcome. Welcome! Come in. I hope you're not in too much of a hurry. Please forgive the mess."

Indeed, his office was a mess, but it was a wonderful home and testimony to a man who truly loved and practiced his profession. Books were strewn about, opened and marked in various places. Jars of anatomical tidbits, of cases past or present, lined shelves. Certificates announcing Gordon Callaway, M.D, and others identifying him as an officer of the court and of the branch of the medical examiner adorned the walls. He thrust a box under my nose and opened it. Inside were fragrant cigars, and he offered me one, which I accepted.

I thanked him and held out the box which Ed had given me.

"This is from Ed."

With a hearty chuckle Dr. Callaway tore into the wrapping like a kid at Christmas. He beamed appreciatively at the contents, also a box of cigars. I knew nothing about cigars, but I knew Ed, and no doubt, these were of exceptional quality.

Gordon smiled and shook his head appreciatively. "Well, well. Give Ed my heartfelt thanks. I'll be sure to call him later. These are my only vice. When I was young and practicing in the military, my mentor smoked cigars during autopsies. No amount of air freshener or disinfectant can get rid of the nasty aura that permeates your pores. My wife hates the pathology smell. Besides, she insists it is easier to get the cigar smell out of the clothes. So let's get on to Laura."

We walked a series of dark corridors and passed through several doors that could only be opened by scanning a sensor with the I.D. card that Dr. Callaway wore clipped to his lapel.

We entered a large room. One wall contained six sliding drawers large enough to house one body each. Their interiors were refrigerated. Dr. Callaway peered up, looking at the name tags, adjusting his bifocals as he did so, and slid open a drawer. He rolled an exam table close and we muscled a shrouded body onto it, and moved it under the lights.

He unzipped the shroud, and I got my first look at Laura.

She had been a beautiful woman. She had the long, lean, well-sculpted legs of a dancer. Her face bore scars, but even they could not hide the fact that she was once quite attractive. Her features were otherwise unremarkable, with the exception of the huge midline incision that advertised the fact that Dr. Callaway had explored her, looking to find the "what" and "why" of her death. We both stared for a minute and shook our heads.

Callaway stepped back to a cabinet, and when he returned he was carrying a box. He opened it and I could feel goose bumps on my flesh for a few seconds. Inside were the faces. The artwork was exquisite. I expected them to talk to me any second. The M.E. removed them and laid them on a shelf.

Callaway spoke softly. "The roommate asked us to think about Laura's life and choose her death mask appropriately. Choose which one you think best defined her in real life. I would like to keep the others."

"How hard did you look at the roommate for this?" I asked.

"We thought she was the most logical suspect. But, you know, I think the D.A. was almost relieved when the inquest came back as suicide. He doesn't want to spend the city's money on a case he might lose. There are just too many unanswered questions surrounding this poor lady. Jeez. I should write a book. Were there fingerprints on the knife? What was the demeanor of the roommate when they found her? Did she have blood on her? Whatever. Not my call. Anyway, got any ideas on the mask we should use?"

We both looked more carefully at each one. "I'm not sure why you're asking me, I really wasn't that intimate with the details. Why not ask the psych guy?"

"Because I hate psychs. I don't trust them. How can you prove in a court of law what a person was thinking? If three people see me smile, each of them will interpret what I am smiling about and why. Each has his own agenda, his own slant. Much like a jury, we try to stack the inquests with people who have no stock in the case. They are usually the least biased. I only ask for the psych's input as a last resort"

I felt a bit guilty listening to his explanation. He wanted my help in choosing a death mask, and I felt guilty for not having listened more attentively to Laura's story. I stared at the masks again. Sad Lisa was out. Lynette had been a disinterested bystander. Leah was the obvious choice. She portrayed the shy, quiet alter ego. Who would not wish to be remembered in that way? "I think I would choose Leah."

"Mmm. I can appreciate that. She thought she was a popular socialite, but perhaps what she really wanted was just to be herself and be accepted for that. Perhaps, in life, Laura could have gotten away with wearing just this one mask."

He boxed up the mask that was Leah and handed it to me. We wheeled Laura out through the large sliding door at the back of the room and loaded her into Carson's SUV.

Later that evening, the crematory claimed Laura. Fire had damaged her spirit at one point. Now the crematory would destroy her body. Perhaps now the fire would set her soul free.

I thought to myself and became melancholy. *I am here to free you from your pain. Fire destroyed you once, now perhaps it can release you from your torment. Be happy. Torment is reserved for the living.*

Many months later, I would remember Laura and this silent conversation. I would be eternally grateful that I had not been able to take her place, and as I was being released from my own torment, I was now capable of grieving for her and others. But for now, I paused before punching the combination of buttons that would start the fires.

Years later I would be reviewing this case and I could imagine Laura speaking. *Remember, Friend, it is much harder to live a lie than to struggle with the truth. Lies last for an eternity. I know this to be true because there is a clown here. We both have plenty of time to relive our torment.*

# Chapter 16:

# This is What It Sounds Like When Heroes Cry

For each memorable case, there were dozens that were forgettable. I was learning that all people are relevant. Memories of some may fade faster than others, but are no less important. Larger than life heroes – movie actors, famous singers, sports figures – are made small by death, the great equalizer. Their accomplishments are forgotten or eclipsed before the grass grows over their graves.

The true hero is the common man. My dead friend, Henny Kaiser, turned into an unwilling and unlikely hero. I will never forget him because he forced the people around him to redefine the important things in this life. He used to say, "If the house you lived in all your life was on fire and you had time to make only two trips inside to retrieve valuables, what would they be? If it all went up in smoke could you survive? Does physical 'stuff' define you?"

Henny totally changed the way I looked at people and the monuments they built to themselves.

Henny also brought Adelina back into my life.

When Henny was first introduced to me in the prep room, I saw a man with an odd- shaped face, big jowls, pouting lips and oversized ears. Built on a short, squat frame, he reminded me of the three simians in the pose "See no evil, Speak no evil and Hear no evil."

Stranger still, Ed came into the room and announced to me that he was personally going to take the case.

Ed gave me sketchy details. "We are going to get Henny here ready for a very expensive casket burial. You and I are going to be officiating one of the largest funerals this city has ever seen."

"Hmmph." I snorted, my ego somewhat bruised that Ed was taking away a case that was obviously very high profile, "Must be some sort of wealthy politician, and people feel they'll have to attend so they can talk about how they were there and who they rubbed shoulders with."

Ed said nothing, but soon I would find that once again, I was way off.

I watched as Ed transformed Henny. I admired his work grudgingly. Ed was still Master of the Game. Skin toner brushed to perfection; richly but appropriately attired; fingers curled around a favorite pipe. Ed was always fond of telling me that the presentation of the dead is every bit as important as the presentation of a new bride or of an infant prior to baptism.

Over the course of the following days, the numerous visitors entering and exiting Ed's office kept him busy, leaving the rest of the staff attempting to piece together the whole story with the woefully inadequate fragments we could gather. Our efforts were somewhat akin to a dog trying to describe a rich banquet after licking the crumbs that fell to the floor.

The staff and I shook hands with the mayor, the state representatives, and a U.S. senator. We were introduced to the clergy who would be officiating.

Henny was ready. His casket was a subdued, caramel bronze. In stark contrast to John Alford, he looked truly at peace. He was leaving nothing undone. The casket was not garish; in fact, he looked comfortable in it, not stuffed in as an afterthought. Ed's expertise or Henny's demeanor?

The funeral was one that I and the City of Portland remember to this day. It was a celebration. Yes, there was an outpouring of genuine grief, but during the eulogies there was laughter, head-nodding and tears. Unlike Mr. Alford, the gentle spirits that danced through the church that day were genuine and palpable. In the end, Henny spoke to the group as a whole, but left a message for the individual as well.

Ed told me they were to expect seven-to eight-hundred people at the service, and possibly people from the movies as well as additional politicians.

From out of nowhere, I received the strangest nudge. It was as if a voice were prompting me. The room was empty but at the time I could have sworn that the voice could be heard by anyone there. I dismissed it at first, but later, I heard it again.

*"Call Adelina."*

*What? Who?*

*"Call Adelina."*

It had been almost a year since I had seen her, back when I helped her with Hal Christensen, but occasionally she would dart in and out of my thoughts. I had spent a lot of time convincing myself it was over, willing it to be so, not wanting to dwell on something I could never have.

But the voice was insistent. I had to do it. Nerves on edge, I found the number to the nursing home and dialed. The voice on the other end told me to hold on while they paged her. I should have hung up, but I didn't.

She came on the line and hesitantly I spoke. "Hi. This is Michael. I met you a while back with Hal..." She never let me finish.

"Hello yourself! I had just about given up on you. What can I do for you?"

I stammered. "I have a somewhat odd request to make. There is going to be quite a large funeral for someone who apparently was quite an important man. My boss, Ed, and I are officiating. They are expecting upwards of eight-hundred people with a number of important dignitaries. I was wondering if you would like to come?"

"Let me get this straight. You are asking me out? To a funeral?"

"That's about the size of it," I said, anticipating the upcoming rejection.

There was silence on the line, but I could hear her breathing. "I'm going to step out on a limb and trust you on this one. Okay, I'll go. Where and when?"

"You'll go? Really? Fantastic! I mean, thanks!" I said with unbridled enthusiasm, and then I caught myself.

"Tomorrow, St. Paul's, eleven o'clock. I'll try to be with you as best I can, but we will be having our duties to fulfill."

"If this isn't the strangest thing," she said. "Just a minute. Let me check something to be sure… Oh good. I have the entire day off, so I guess I'll see you there. Why are you asking me to a funeral, of all things?"

I struggled for an answer. "The man was a well-known movie critic and had quite a large syndicated newspaper column, so there probably will be a number of well-known people there to pay their respects, possibly even from the movies. Maybe there will be some interesting eulogies. Heck. I really don't know."

"That's not much of an endearing way to ask a girl out," she laughed.

Then she was silent. "I don't know why, but I guess I'm just going to have to step out in faith. I'll see you tomorrow."

I hung up, elated. My feelings were genuine, and how good it felt! I hid nothing. I shook my head in amazement at how much of a thrill I was getting just in hearing her voice. It didn't even bug me when she said something about "faith." I had been with her two or three times, but each time I had felt at peace. If we ever were to meet again outside of work… who knows? I might even pray at a restaurant in public.

The following day Ed and I arrived at the church more than an hour early only to find the church was almost full. I still had no real idea who Henny Kaiser had been in life, other than what Ed had told me. The pastor met with us and was all smiles. Ed had checked the arrangements in his usual thorough fashion, and there was no rush, no last minute scurrying about.

After meeting with the pastor, I lost track of Ed. I caught occasional glimpses of him speaking with a number of people. He was enjoying the crowd, but I was bored. Hundreds of people there and I knew no one.

Then I spotted Adelina…and so did everybody else.

She was wearing a sky-blue dress that reached just below her knees. The skirt portion was light enough to flow gently when she moved, but did not cling to her. Her dark hair reached almost to the middle of her back, and she had pinned each side up off her ears. It was my job to notice makeup, and she had applied hers with perfection, just enough to let the viewer know she was using something, but not so much as to cause a distraction.

Her natural beauty was the envy of queens. She drew a crowd wherever she went, and it was obvious she was a bit uneasy with it all.

I could see that people were trying to engage her in conversation, but she only stared back at them, timid or frightened, I couldn't tell which. I reached her and touched her on the elbow. She whirled around, ready to face the new intrusion. When she recognized me, she visibly relaxed.

"Oh. Hi. Am I glad to see you."

I stood speechless for a few seconds, and then said in a quiet voice, "You are beautiful."

She blushed and smiled, and said "Thank you. Now tell me. What is this all about?"

"The deceased man is Henny Kaiser. He was some big shot guy who wrote about famous people. Ed would not really tell me a lot. He is actually the lead on this case. All this was done with him at the helm."

I waved an arm at the preparations. Once again, the private florists had provided a magnificent array of fresh flowers. The church was huge, and there were still twenty minutes before the service would start, but it was packed. There were two large public address speakers set out on the front steps, so those who could not find a seat inside would hear the service.

I noticed that many in the crowd were not dressed in requisite formal dark clothes. Some came very casual. There were older people, and unless I missed my guess, quite a number of the city's homeless. The pastor smiled and engaged all of them. No one would be turned away. All manner of mankind was represented here today, and lots of them.

By the time the pastor was ready with his opening remarks, the crowd had swelled, spilling into the front patio almost into the street. Inside was standing room only. Two news channels covered the proceedings and worked the crowd. I wondered, *Who was this man?*

I escorted Adelina to a spot in the back, and apologized to her, as she would have to be standing for the majority of the memorial.

"That's okay," she said, "Now I am too curious to leave."

The service began with a brief prayer. The pastor looked out at the expectant gathering and took a deep breath. "Today is a day for the affirmation of the beautiful life of Henny Kaiser. We all knew him, but I am going to step down and let those who wish to speak come and fill in the blanks. I would like to give my address, but what I have to say can wait. By the end of the day, those of you who didn't know Henny well, will begin to understand why we are all here, paying tribute; although the very thought of these formalities would horrify him. We have all day, so don't be shy."

There was a pause and general murmuring coursed through the church. Everyone, it seemed, had some tidbit they wanted to share, and by my estimate, there were more than seven hundred in the audience. Several people stood up to move forward, but when a lady in the front rose, the others sat again, out of respect. I wasn't sure how they knew, but the lady was Henny's wife. She slowly ascended the few stairs and reached the lectern. Her words came from a woman mourning, but also reflected what had been, and what was to come. She had a message from Henny, and she wanted to make sure she got it just right. She took to the pulpit and began.

"There was no getting over it. Henny was just plain ugly." She walked down to the closed casket and touched it gently, and said "Sorry, my love, but it's the truth."

The crowd laughed and there was a smattering of applause. Eleven well-placed words and seven-hundred people embraced her.

She chuckled, perhaps a bit more relaxed, sensing the crowd's acceptance. "He wasn't good at much. He never had too many friends in high school. His looks made him the brunt of many cruel jokes. When he was near, people snickered. He assumed they were talking about him, and usually, he was right. He had never been taunted to fight, but he told me he almost wished he had. He would have rather suffered the physical abuse than being ostracized."

She paused to let her words take effect. The people in the assembly murmured and nodded in agreement, themselves very well acquainted with the grief one human can pile on another because they were branded as "different."

"Soon people tired of him and he was ignored. His grades were quite good. After all, with no social life, what else was there to do? Slowly, things began to change. He discovered since he was a source for derision and laughter, he could turn that around in his favor. He began to poke fun at himself. People laughed but they let him be. He took a huge gamble and began speaking; first at small gatherings, then giving more formal speeches whenever opportunities arose. It was always the same theme – he would present himself as the consummate fall guy for the common man. It is said that ugly, reclusive people make the best comedians. He proved that."

126

There was polite laughter.

"After a bit, he steered away from a strictly comic venue and became a popular all- around speaker. He loved making motivational speeches. Now people laughed with him, not at him. More importantly, people identified with him. He went on to graduate from a prestigious college, and never missed an opportunity to give a talk. If he was unfamiliar with the topic, he would advertise himself as an expert, and then study until he truly became somewhat of an expert.

"To all of you out there, whether or not I know your names. You are my friends and I do not wish to wax nostalgic and get teary-eyed." Her voice cracked. "There will be plenty of time for that. But for now, there are others here that wish to continue the timeline."

Then she was finished. For a moment, the facade of this lovely lady cracked. She looked around, not sure of what to do next, and tried to catch herself in an attempt not to weep. Almost as if on cue, the entire congregation stood and applauded. The energy of the crowd caught her. She lifted her head and smiled. She waved and sat down. It was as genuine an outpouring of affection as I had ever seen. I watched as this mass of people let their guard down. I looked at Adelina, then the crowd, and thought "there is no place I would rather be, must be, than right here, right now."

From the back of the church, a heavy man made his way slowly toward the front.

He nodded and smiled at a few people as he reached the last few rows of pews and ascended to the dais.

"Good morning. My name is David Morefield and I am the owner of the *Metro Tribune*."

There was a brief period of conversation as the introduction and recognition set in. *Portland Metro* was the city's largest newspaper. I did not read the papers much. When I did, I skimmed headlines and sports. The name Henny Kaiser still meant nothing to me.

"I would like to tell you how I immediately discovered Henny's writing talents, but that would be a lie. His speaking talents naturally evolved into writing, but his first submissions were marginal, at best. He finally managed to secure a regular column with one of our competitors. Soon he became syndicated in many newspapers throughout the country. Due to my personal lack of foresight, ours was one of the last papers to pick him up.

"Readers valued Henny's opinion, and the social climbers loved the press coverage. To have their names alongside his provided a huge career boost, or afforded a springboard to new talent. So, my friends, thanks for letting me be a small part of this. I was honored. Henny was my hero."

Mr. Morefield sat down and there was a pause. Then another murmur began quietly at first, then a crescendo, then something just short of pandemonium. Adelina gasped in recognition and put her hand to her mouth in surprise.

George Blandino, a handsome black man walked down the center aisle and took his place to speak. I immediately perked up and became more attentive. George Blandino was one of the finest and best known movie actors currently on the big screen. Just what in the heck was he doing here? This funeral had been in progress for about twenty minutes and there were several quite famous people present, waiting to pay their respects to a man I had never heard of.

When the din finally settled, George began. "Good morning. My name is George. *(polite laughter)* "I met Henny probably ten years ago. In my own mind I thought I was a great actor and very popular. But of course, I had a distorted, misplaced sense of my own worth. I had no problem playing characters that were immoral, dishonest, filthy and lewd, especially when there was money to be made, and recognition to be had.

"Henny used to write for a Hollywood entertainment magazine that had a huge circulation. He featured me in his column a few times and I loved it. I begged him to write about me every so often, because as long as the famous Henny Kaiser had me in his sights, I made money. I wasn't the only one. All of us stars loved him, but, you know, love is fickle. As long as the stars were in his column, we were his friends. As for me, to forget me was to be forgotten by me. The press is omnipotent. I knew it, Henny knew it. All of Hollywood knew it. When he failed to write about us, we forgot he existed. Friendship was a one-way street.

"I became a leech. Henny was always surrounded by sycophants. They all wanted a piece of him. We were all takers; no one ever gave. One day Henny announced he was taking a break from writing due to 'exhaustion.' He stopped giving, but we wanted more anyway. When we found out we couldn't have him, we abandoned him. No one called on him. No one came to check on his welfare. Not one of us 'superstars' would Henny ever be able to call 'his hero.' I lost touch with him for several years and when I found him again, it was because I went out and looked for him."

At this point George Blandino, famous actor, cried real tears. An uncomfortable pall fell over the crowd, no one sure of just quite what to do.

Blandino walked to the casket and touched the edge. "I looked for you, Henny," he sobbed. "Really I did."

Finally the pastor came up, put his arm around his shoulder, and led him to a chair off to one side. The pastor reclaimed the pulpit and he brought the remaining pieces of Henny's life together.

"I met Henny by accident at a restaurant that was frequented by movie stars. He used to eat there in the hopes of catching a glimpse of someone famous to write about for his next column. He seemed very depressed. We struck up a conversation. The conversation and the friendship lasted a lifetime. He felt sorry for himself. He had been appreciated for a price and the price was too great. He felt he should quit writing and find some solitude for a time. During his months of depression and self-imposed loneliness, life went on. Terrorism; a new war overseas. He lived in a spacious penthouse in a big city but even that could not drown out the sirens he heard almost every night."

At this, the pastor paused and looked around the audience. He called out. "Cliff? Did Clifford Kennedy make it?"

People craned their necks in order to get a glimpse of someone. Who, no one knew, but if it had anything to do with Henny Kaiser he must be famous. Finally, close to the back of the church, people focused on a man standing. He looked to be in his late twenties. There was nothing too remarkable about him, except he had only one arm. The other had been severed just above the elbow. He said nothing and sat back down.

Again numerous "Shhhs!!" could be heard as people strained to hear. The pastor continued.

"Clifford Kennedy was discharged from the U.S. Marines. While on patrol in Viet Nam, he accidently sprang a booby trap that took his arm off. He too was feeling sorry for himself. He met Henny, and both their lives changed in an instant. I invited him to tell his story but he is giving me the honor and pleasure of allowing me to do it. Cliff, I hope I do you justice. Let me take a step back here.

"Henny finally tired of being a recluse and had decided to return to work. He tried, but he no longer had a passion to write about the selfish, spoiled, overpaid brats that America considered its heroes."

He turned to face George, still on the platform in the same seat, and smiled at him.

"Sorry, my friend. "

"Anyway, walking home one evening, Henny heard what sounded like someone crying. He looked for the source of the sound and saw an old man hugging a young man, in front of a homeless shelter. The old man was in tears. The young man was Cliff, and the older man had been a Marine in the last 'war-to-end-all-wars' and was thanking him for his service in the only way he knew how, for he knew that the young man had sacrificed much more than an arm.

"Henny waited for the two to part, and he met Cliff, who filled him in on what had just transpired. Cliff had been walking the streets that night, trying to find a secluded spot where he could take his own life, where no one would intrude and frustrate his plans. Unknown to the old veteran, he saved Cliff's life that night by giving him back his self-worth. Cliff and Henny remained friends.

"Henny told me he went home that night and wept. Later, he collected his thoughts, and the floodgates opened. He finally had a real story to tell, a story about true heroes. These men in their respective generations had quietly gone about their business so we, in our depravity could have the freedom to elevate America's so-called superstars to a place they didn't deserve. Henny remembered. He had made quite an impact with his audiences by poking fun at the common man. Now that common man would be the focus of his writing. He could write about them because he could identify with them.

"The story about the sacrifice of the two Marines went unnoticed for a while, but the name Henny Kaiser still carried clout. One night, a major TV news program told Cliff's story as a human interest bit as they were signing off. The station was flooded with calls and mail. People wanted more. Henny submitted a few similar stories, and soon he was again the talk of dozens of major wire services in America. But now he turned to the unsung heroes.

"The single parent working two jobs so his/her child could be the first in a generation to be college educated. The fireman who pulled a panicked woman from a burning building, then disappeared to avoid publicity. The people who go to work each day to ensure Americans could take advantage of the intangibles so often taken for granted – freedom of the press, freedom of thought, all for a nation full of self-serving, callous people that deserved much less.

"His name and column quickly became a household staple. The public admired him for his strength of character and the courage of his convictions. He would always tell people, 'If imitation is the highest form of flattery, then you need to become what you think I am.'

"He opened a deep gash in the soft underbelly of a nation that has never healed, and he poured salt in it…"

At this, much of the audience stood, and cheers and applause filled the church.

The pastor was almost shouting now, "…and Henny was loved for it! He wrote that the common man had no skin color, desired frankness and honesty from elected leaders, wanted boundaries set, and would not tolerate compromise!"

Pandemonium set in. The pastor could have announced he was running for president, and the crowd would have carried him on their shoulders all the way to the White House.

Another man approached the podium and whispered a few words to the pastor. The pastor motioned for silence, and a moment later, he could speak again. "This is Mr. Voyle Beers. He is the senior editor of the *San Francisco Daily Journal News*. He would like to deliver the final eulogy."

"Good morning. I would like to read you one of the last columns Henny wrote. I clipped it and keep it with me at all times.

"'America. Today I poke you at your conscience. How dare you worship people who make millions only so they can appear on national television and deride the very nation that made them rich? How dare you encourage your children to emulate the liars, cheaters and drug-abusing sports stars who will trample anyone who stands in the way of their next goal, whose signature on a contract is less than worthless? When will we become so ashamed of the filth masquerading as music that is poisoning children every day that we will cry 'Enough!' When will we realize the real stars, the real heroes, are not the millionaires who sit in judges' chambers and overturn laws that are meant to keep our morality in check, but the police, fire, and others who work for pennies a day? They leave their homes and their families every morning wondering if they will return at night. How about the nurses caring for those we have no more use for? The elderly? The dying? The imperfect children whom we dismiss as disposable? Nurses don't show up to work every morning in a limousine as photographers snap every step.

"No, Mr. Common Man. You will never be rich or famous, but you will be an unsung superstar. Go to your homes. Love your families. Kiss your children. Talk to and learn from the dying. Be there as they slip into immortality. Those that trip and fall in your path did so for a reason. The mark of the finest human being is to bend down and help them. America, I don't want to be your hero. I want each of you to be my hero.'"

With that he was finished. I half expected the place to go crazy again, but everyone kept their seats, and many were sobbing. Mr. Beers reclaimed his seat and for a few moments there was no motion, and very little noise. All were waiting expectantly, but for what?

Then, the strangest thing happened, and Hollywood could not have choreographed it any better. George Blandino got out of his seat and stood on his chair. He said loudly, "Henny, I am your hero!"

There was a pause, and everyone looked about in confusion, not knowing what to expect next. Several seconds passed and someone stood in a pew and shouted, "Henny, I am your hero!" Beginning slowly at first, and then with a clamor, people all over the church stood up and proclaimed themselves to be Henny's hero. The chant carried into the churchyard and continued there. Acknowledging that one was Henny's hero was becoming, for the common man, a catch phrase.

Unofficially or otherwise, the service came to an end. I imagine that many more people could have given their testimonies of the impact Henny had had on their lives, but the huge audience began to disperse, so they would never get the chance. I guided Adelina out to the front of the church and we walked slowly toward her car.

"Well, what did you think?" I asked.

"It was beautiful. He must have said so much in his lifetime that most of us wish we could say, and he lived it too."

I nodded in agreement. "Where would this country be if just half the people practiced the morality they say they believe in? Would young people going off to war feel better about fighting for a nation that values common decency? I fought in a war. Would I be as willing to fight for the American way of life as it is now? We need to be brought back to a sense that there is such a thing as right and wrong, and sometimes there is no gray area."

132

Adelina looked up at me and smiled. "Do you really feel that way or are you just saying that?"

I looked at my feet sheepishly. I glanced sideways at her. I thought, You are not as naive as you let on. You can see right through me. "I suppose I deserved that," I said. "Ed has been nudging me to learn from the people I meet, learn of their failures and their successes. All I can say is, I'm learning a lot about myself and I am changing. It is turning out to be a wild but enjoyable ride."

She smiled and took my hand and gave it a gentle squeeze. We reached her car. "Perhaps there is hope for you yet." She took a few steps away, her back to me. She reached for the handle of the car door and turned. I was surprised as she reached out and gently touched my cheek with a finger, letting it linger. "Maybe the mask is coming off. Call me sometime?"

She pressed a crumpled piece of paper in my hand.

I watched as she drove off, then peered at the paper. On it was written a phone number. I positively glided on air back to the church.

Much later, the crowd thinned but many were still passing by to take one last glimpse of Henny. Ed had opened the top half of the casket for viewing, and as he noticed me reentering the church he waved me over.

"Well, I think we're about ready to wrap this up. Can you finish with Henny, and I'll meet you in a bit? Oh. Can you wipe that smile off your face? This is supposed to be a somber occasion" Then he was off again, looking back at me with a grin of his own.

I waited a few more minutes and closed the lid of the coffin over Henny and looked about. There were still quite a number of people clustered in small groups visiting, but all who wanted to view him had come and gone. The only dignitary I would have wanted to meet was George Blandino, but undoubtedly, he had been spirited away. I sighed as I looked at the closed box containing Henny.

*Would he have approved of all that had just transpired? Would I, Michael Alexander, be on Henny's list of heroes?*

Ed and I rode to the gravesite. I enjoyed the time together because Ed spoke to me as a friend and a peer. We arrived at the cemetery and maneuvered the casket onto a rolling cart and placed it near Henny's appointed resting place.

The sexton came with his backhoe and opened the earth. After he finished, Ed and I surveyed his handy work. The earth looked as if it resisted this horrible intrusion. It was an unwilling participant, not yet ready to receive the likes of this beautiful man.

And so it was that this great man (who refused that particular title), was laid to rest. His funeral was indeed the largest Portland had seen in quite some time. There were hundreds of common people in attendance, but more importantly, they shared a common bond.

I threw a single flower on top of the casket just before Henny was commended and consigned forever. As it hit the casket, I bowed my head and whispered so only Henny could hear, "Henny, can I be your hero?"

*Adelina, I loved you the first day I met you. Irma and Henny will be on my list of people to hug if I ever make it to where you are. We were married almost 50 years but the courtship never ended. Was ever a creature put on this earth that had a heart like yours?* ...the musings of an old man. How does one measure the quality of a heart? I'm sure many people would have a mate or best friend in mind that was just as close to them as we had been. But I am old and this is my story, so I can go on about my beloved. And should death come for me tomorrow and these words never be read, then that's okay too, because it will eventually be known for all eternity. And there are no tomorrows in eternity.

How does one measure the goodness of a heart? Can we weigh it? Can we open it up and shine a light into it and force it to give up its secrets? No. Puny, simple man cannot, but love can.

Sitting in my study and daydreaming, I remember certain cases, certain lessons I want to pass onto my children, should they be willing to take the time and read and learn from them.

I get melancholy, thinking about Adelina.

*Hey, Honey, did I ever tell you about a girl named Natalie and the goodness of her heart? Perhaps love can be measured. Look over my shoulder and read this... perhaps you have even met her and her father by now.*

# Chapter 17:
# The Death of Mediocrity

It is the cool of the evening. I am at the mausoleum where Adelina lies. It has been awhile since I talked with her, and I will do so tonight, until it turns dark.

*Hey, Sweetie, I want to be where you are, but how can I be sure? You told me you were sure before you left me. How did you know? Were you right?*

I drift off during these conversations as I am apt to do, and I hear her voice. Her voice takes me back to another time. Years ago, countless conversations ago.

*Darling,* I hear her say, *remember the story you told me about Emma Jean? How did she know? What was her assurance? Unfortunately for you, my love, there are some questions you must answer for yourself. Hard questions. But don't wait too long...*

At home that night, I flipped through files and I found it. Not an answer, not enlightenment, not assurance, but a story. A story my dead friend Emma Jean told me.

The spirit of Emma Jean was introduced to us by the pastor of her church. Her body had arrived at Carson's that morning. She was an elderly lady, looking to be about ninety at the time of death. She was scheduled for a viewing and cremation. When Ed gave me the case, he insisted that I make a social call on her pastor.

I called on the senior pastor of a medium-sized community church. The outside was the stereotypical white building with the cross on the steeple. Inside was a tasteful, quaint sanctuary with the usual wooden pews and somber atmosphere.

I didn't stay lost in my thoughts for long before a man of about sixty, well-built for his age, came through a door, his hard-soled shoes echoing off wooden walls.

I walked toward him; we shook hands and made informal introductions and he led me to an office.

"Thanks for seeing me," I began. "Ed, my boss, thought you could give me some insight into the life of one of your parishioners. Her name was Emma Jean."

"Ah, yes. Emma Jean," he said with a fondness in his voice and his smile. "By the way, how's Ed? I really do have to get out and see him sometime. Is he ever going to retire?"

"You know Ed," I grinned, "if he had his way, we'd find him slumped over at his desk one morning. He loves his job, but I do believe his retirement is imminent."

"Well, I know how that goes. I've been telling myself the same thing for years. But I too have grown to love what I do but, you know, we all have our demons chasing us, fear of being forgotten, fear of the unknown, fear of losing self-worth… Now, about our lady friend."

He breathed a long sigh and leaned back in a tattered chair on wheels that I worried would tilt backward and eventually fall.

"How long have you been at your job?"

I had to think. "Mmm… almost thirty years now.

"Ah. Good. I hope you have found as much fulfillment in your job as Ed and I have in ours. I met Ed a while back and we hit it off almost immediately. He asks tough questions that have no good answers. Very enjoyable. You know, the art of good conversation is dead. There is no depth in most people. No one wants to learn for the sake of learning. Ed has the same outlook on the sorry condition of mankind as I do, although you would never know it.           Do we wish humanity well? Of course. Do we hold out much hope? No."

I sighed deeply, not knowing quite how to phrase my sentiments, or even if I should, to a total stranger. "I have to admit that what worries me the most is whether or not that very perception is what most people are thinking about me. Should I look at the world with hope or despair? Have I as an individual – have we as a race – reached the point of no return? We are sending our young people off to war to preserve... what?... this decadent way of life?"

The pastor shook his head sadly. "If it's any consolation, you don't have a monopoly on that line of thought. Ed and I were just like you. You will never sleep easily until you have some sort of assurance that mankind can never give you. To put it bluntly, your peace and contentment will not come from this world. In my case, I looked around me at all the hate, disgust and filth in the world, and realized that I was the only person getting the ulcer. Are you married?"

I brightened up considerably. "Yes, to a wonderful girl, Adelina, who wants to make a Christian man out of me... but I love her anyway. (He didn't smile at my lame attempt at humor.) She says the same things you do, but keeps warning me that time is short.

Tell me, though... you found a lot of reasons to lose faith. Why didn't you?"

"I finally got to the point where I understood that you have to shovel through a lot of manure to find a bright flower, and when you do, wow! It is worth the trouble... or think about this... What woman going through labor pains remembers only the pains and downplays the joy of the birth? A prize fighter has to subject himself to a lot of blows before he can get in and deal a knockout punch. I learned that everyone is worth my effort, no matter how they respond. True, many people repay kindness with deceit. But I am ecstatic nonetheless. I cherish the blessings and riches I have received from a few people who really can see the light, and I see how their changes far outweigh the garbage I have received from the majority. Man, what a rush!"

"So," I finally asked, "why am I here?"

"Ed almost took this case himself. A few months ago, we sat here for over an hour talking about Emma Jean, and he somewhat casually asked me that should she choose Carson's to do her final arrangements, would I call him personally. As luck would have it, she did end up using Carson's. I'm not sure why Ed gave Emma to you, but he must see something in you that's worth saving."

I snorted. "You and Adelina could trade places, and no one would be the wiser."

"Well, young man, do a good job on Emma Jean. I would like to see her again and there are a number of parishioners who will most assuredly drop in. I've seen Ed's work and you have big shoes to fill.

I am going to tell you a story about Ed, and I am going to trust you not to repeat it. Please... for my sake and Ed's, don't tell him I told you this. I am only telling you as to give you an insight into a person that I for one, think is a great man.

"Years ago, there was a teenaged girl all dressed up for a school field trip, waiting on a corner for a ride with some friends. She never made it to school. She was abducted, raped, and her skull mercifully, but brutally, bashed to pieces. Most funeral directors would have just consigned her to a closed-casket/no-viewing, and gone home for the night.

"Ed spent almost an entire twenty-four hours reconstructing her face and skull. He dressed her, cleaned her hands and washed her hair. He was so emotionally exhausted that he was on the verge of tears. He did cry with the family, and later, after he came to grips with his own angst, he told me that it had all been worth it. That little girl had helped him slay a lot of his demons. The look on the family's face when they saw how beautiful their little girl was is probably what saved Ed's sanity, if not his life.

"I saw her before and after. It was a masterful God-given re-creation. It was easier for that family to grieve, because they could actually see the object of their grief. It was a turning point for him, because he found purpose in his work. Ed is a man who truly practices what he preaches. You should be honored he is giving you a case that he wants.

"Now, on to the story of Emma Jean before I go off on another tangent.

"I have a B.A. in religious apologetics. I speak four languages. Emma Jean taught me more in two years than I could learn with a dozen degrees. She had been a lukewarm churchgoer for years. Her husband died awhile back and after his death she attended even less often. She kept quiet and stayed to herself. I never saw her chatting with anyone.

"One Sunday, she came in positively radiant. I had to do a double-take because I didn't recognize her. After service, when I was greeting people, she came up to me and said, "'You don't recognize me, do you?'

"I smiled and shook my head and replied, 'No, not in the least.'

"'Well, my name is Emma Jean and I have a story to tell.'

"We made a date for Monday, the following day."

I rose from my chair and walked about a bit to get the stiffness out of my aching hips. I glanced at my watch. No wonder. I had been sitting in this awkward wooden chair for forty-five minutes already.

138

"Sorry," he chuckled, not seeming to notice my discomfort, "this is a magnificent story and I have to tell it my way. Actually, I am practicing on you because I am writing it into a sermon."

"Okay," I said. "I'll make you a deal. I am your toughest critic. If I think your story has merit, I'll listen to the sermon."

His eyes lit up. "That's the beauty of it! It is not my story! It is not really even her story. You don't – no, you can't – exude the kind of passion and use the words that she did without an incredible personal experience that some might call being filled with the Holy Spirit. Call it what you will. Come and listen, but not because you made a bet."

Then he chuckled and added, "Which you are about to lose.

"So Monday came and she was prompt. She could hardly contain herself. I am going to try to relate this as close to what she said as I can.

"'My name is Emma Jean, and a few years ago I went to the military cemetery where my husband is buried because I was going to kill myself next to his grave. I figured I would take a large dose of poison and collapse near his marker. At least they would know with whom to bury me.

"'I really did not have a good reason to die, but then again, I didn't have a good reason to live, either. I was a widow. I had no friends. I came here, and no one noticed me. We had no money. Our marriage produced no children. I never had visitors. That day I made it to the cemetery and was somewhat annoyed. I usually park in the bottom lot because my husband's grave is near there. But there was some sort of construction going on, and it forced me to park in the upper lot, which meant a bit of a walk.

"'I remember looking out over the graves on the hillside and for the first time seeing hundreds upon hundreds of evenly-spaced rows of crosses, white on a green backdrop. I was pleased and somewhat relieved with an odd rationalization. I had finally found a reason to kill myself! I'm sure there was well over a thousand crosses there, all those graves. .. all occupied with the same forgotten, plain, boring people. What difference would one more plain, boring person make?

"'I started down the slope to where Al, my husband, lay. On the way, I read some of the inscriptions, which only strengthened my desire to end it all.

"'–Here lies M. Dorsey. Died a spinster...'

"'–This is the grave of Father Sprague. He delivered hundreds of homilies...'

"'–Here lies Malcolm DeWitt. Born 1953. Killed in action 1971...'

"'Don't you see? The theme was the same – hopelessness, despair, loneliness. Lots of lives lived, lots lost, most that no one cared about. I passed through dead after dead. I could feel their burdens, their bitter disappointments; job interviews with never a call back. Some never had the luxury of being jilted lovers; they had never even been loved; not getting a part in a play that might have launched a career.

"'The markers cried out,' We failed! Why should you be any different from the rest of us? We all died without causes, without purposes. No one noticed us, no one noticed our passing. We were rich, no one cared. We were young, no one listened. We were athletes, forgotten as soon as our records fell. We were poor, and they sneered. We were not fair of feature to look upon and we were shunned. What pride we had, they waited until we left and they even stripped us of that. Wealth and fame are fleeting; deceit and manipulation are the order of the day.

"'Emma Jean! We await you!"

At this point, the pastor removed his glasses and wiped them dry before continuing. I had begun this discussion by listening, convinced I could remain ambivalent. Now I was riveted, transported inside the mind of Emma Jean, not wanting to leave until she finished with me.

"At this point," the pastor continued, "Emma Jean started to cry. She had me hooked and I was mentally urging her to finish her story. Finally she did.

"'By the time I reached Al, I was totally exhausted mentally. I had the strength of purpose to reach into my purse, pull out the pill bottles, and take the lid off. But for some reason, the first pill got stuck in the neck of the bottle and I had to tip my head way back in an attempt to get it out. With my head tilted back, I caught a glimpse of a beautiful array of flowers at someone's marker. I lowered the bottle to look. It was so colorful against this field of white. I went over, and bent down to touch them. The voices crying out were different this time.

"'Here lies a poor, indifferent soul. Why is he unique? He is not. He is mediocre, unloved by man, but he didn't care. He knew that a Greater Being, no less than the God of the universe, loved him. He knew he was loved, and he had been promised eternity by the very Creator of all! That was more important than the accolades of men.

Failure is fleeting. Caring is eternal. Where in the universe would he rather be than where he is now? In the palm of the Maker's hand!'"

Again the man stopped, and this time I watched as his eyes drifted off to a place where I was not invited.

He picked up again. "A defining moment of her life was a point that I should have been involved in, but was not, and I regret it to this day. She told me that the words of another pastor came to her. A seed planted so many years ago sprang to existence to its fullest grandeur in the most critical instant of her life.

"'Two thousand years ago a man lived. Those who believed He lived and lives still, live a life of blessed hope and renewal. Theirs is the assurance of eternal security, wealth, and happiness.'

"Emma Jean finished by telling me that she rose up from her knees and she finally knew. There was indeed a death on a cross many years ago. It was the death of mediocrity."

He was finished, and neither of us spoke. It was time standing still for both of us.

We finally stood up and he ushered me to the door. "The most compelling proof that a relationship with God exists is people like Emma Jean... a changed life. She began to smile. She made it a point to get to know people, sharing their triumphs and tragedies. People began to confide in her because she was genuine. She maintained this high energy and passion for years, up until the very time of her death. At her death, the outpouring of grief and the celebration of life was shared by the entire congregation.

"I think it was a powerful missionary who once said, "Don't consider it folly to lose what you can't keep, in order to gain something you can't lose."

"Emma knew. Emma knew."

He stood up and ushered me to the door. The sanctuary echoed my footsteps. A fitting backdrop for my thoughts.

I left the church understanding and appreciating the life and faith of this lady. I returned to Carson's and began her preparation. I was ready to give Emma Jean the best. I was ready to dress her in a beautiful gown. I was ready to color her hair and set it in the latest style. I was ready to take years off her face. And I heard Mr. Thomas chuckling.

"Hey, Michael. That just wouldn't be Emma Jean, would it?"

Emma Jean's pastor was one of those enviable people who,

repeatedly being forged on life's anvil, emerged stronger and more committed to what he defined as his faith. He had not run away from his God bitter and whining just because at times he felt he wasn't getting a fair shake. He and Ed personified what I hoped someday to become.

Emma Jean had dozens of people show up to pay their respects. Ed came, mostly to laugh with his old friend. If he was pleased with Emma's presentation, he didn't let on.

After the last mourner left, Ed and the pastor stayed behind. He didn't flinch as we placed Emma gently in a paper box. He shook his head sadly as we slowly and reverently rolled her into the crematory.

She was ninety, and in her passing, there was genuine grief. As the pastor turned to leave he left us with a rhetorical question, with his answer. "When was the right time to die? When you and your Creator decide you are ready. A life is never cut short. It is completed."

*So that's where Ed got that phrase!*

He looked at us, composed now, and perhaps for a moment felt the need to step into a familiar role, perhaps stand behind a welcoming pulpit, whatever. Perhaps it was a parting eulogy. "You know, the only light worth a darn is a light that after it goes out, can still be seen a bit. Look at the moon. The sun gives light, the moon receives it.

'Emma was that way. She was a light, and now that she is gone, others have taken the light she gave and are shining… including her pastor. See you in church, Son!" Then he was gone.

*My darling Michael...* I was sitting with Adelina again.
*The pastor tells me he didn't gain a convert, but I saw you that Sunday sneaking in to his church, way in the back. What he says is true! Come to me before it is too late. You heard his sermon. He is anxious for you. Irma Glendale knows the words he spoke. Misha Kloski as well. Give up readily that which you can't keep!*

*Adelina my love! I'm trying, really I am. I have doubts. I have fears. Will I ever be good enough? It seems like I am a dog paddling in the water, going nowhere. How will I know?*

142

# Chapter 18:
# Forgive Us Our Debts

The funeral business has been very good for me. I look back over almost forty years. I made great friends, living and dead.

Oh… about that turtle on the fence post? Perhaps he's ready to be lifted to the next higher level.

I needed a lot of help getting to where I am today. Ed, my boss, mentor and friend retired a few years back. He was a rare find in this day and age; honest and ethical and intolerable of anyone in the profession who was not. At his retiring, he opened up his files and shared stories of some of his memorable cases. At a dinner given for him, he let us in on some of the people living and dead that guided and shaped him through the years. I was amazed. He was like the country doctor who treated many patients – the "famous" people he had met! the generations; the families he buried; the people he grieved with and for. Many sought him out when they had burdens they knew he would be willing to help them carry. Death is no respecter of class or money. It makes a visit to all. Ed just happened to have a knack for helping the survivors through the dark times, and they remembered and loved him for it. They would have done anything for him, but he never asked.

Quite possibly the greatest legacy he (or anyone else for that matter) left me was a bit of advice.

"You've seen the living; you are familiar with the dead. Do you want to round out your career and get a real measure of your inner feelings? Visit a few people who have just received a death sentence. Perhaps it is from their doctor. Perhaps they have decided to commit suicide over a broken relationship or whatever. Perhaps they have been given a life sentence behind bars. Perhaps they are in a hospital forgotten by all except for the machines that keep them alive.

"Visit them. Talk with them. Sit quietly, if necessary, and witness the transition... the transition between life and death. Watch those who have lived a 'good' life and are about to succumb to a terminal illness; sit with a family in an emergency room lobby waiting for the doors to open, admitting the man in the white smock who approaches to tell them what they already know: their young son is almost dead, the innocent victim of a crime. Watch as time stands still.

"Notice the difference in the hand. The hand of the dying person who has given in to the inevitable and awaits the next phase in peace, versus the hand of the person struggling to hold on. Notice the hand of someone who embraces faith; the hand of someone who wants to live just so they can postpone eternal damnation because they don't know how to avoid it; the hand that clutches yours with the fear of the unknown."

*Hey, Ed. I should have told you. I took your advice. I swear, I think I cried more than the families did. I wish I had been with you at your death. I only wish I will be able to handle my death as gracefully as I bet that you did.*

*Have you seen my Adelina? Has she told you? Has this dear person told you about what we went through? Did she tell you that without your advice I never would have made it through her death? Did she tell you about her stroke and how she wanted a quick, merciful passing so I wouldn't have to see her in her debilitated condition? Did she tell you that I wouldn't give her permission to go? That I wanted to selfishly keep her for myself, no matter how horrible it must have been for her?*

And I heard Ed talking to me. *Michael. Don't you get it by now? Don't you understand that Adelina and I do not talk about pain and suffering and physical death because we are in a place where all that does not exist?*

*Can I give you some advice? What is the most common regret that dying people have? What do all people want and need? What is the one thing that when we all get it, allows us to go into eternity with joy? What is the one thing that you need the most, are searching for the most, but in reality is yours to give?*

144

*Look in the files. Sit with a boy named Sammy Cruz. Take a moment to remember the story of Raymond Massey. Learn from them...*

What drives people to suicide and what drives others to keep struggling against insurmountable odds are questions that are not answerable in this life. One of my dead friends spent six years in a Vietnamese prisoner of war camp, isolated in a four-foot-by-five-foot room, enduring unspeakable torture and survived to live a productive life."

Suffice it to say that, in this business, all of our morticians have seen many youngsters, teenagers mostly, end their lives over something as trivial as puppy love. They have lost their first love and are convinced there will never be another.

Much of the funeral director's job is to listen. So many people tell us everything that, in reality, they should have told the deceased during their life. Many feel if they unload this private grief on us, they will somehow be absolved of their guilt. This is never the case. We are not given the power to forgive a person's regrets. The person must forgive himself. Only then are they ready to let go... to move on in peace.

The man on the table was almost sixty. He would be cremated. Death had released him, we hoped, from a private hell. The expression on his face did not appear peaceful or tormented. Rather, it looked resigned. After his mother told us his story, I wondered if the fires of the crematory would be hot enough, and purge thoroughly enough, a most forgettable and regrettable life.

Sammy Cruz had always been the class clown, his mother explained, and this was duly noted. If someone made a joke, he would try to top it. If there was a practical joke to be played, Sammy was usually the one behind it. He was the terror of the fourth grade.

She said it really was not all his fault. You have to understand... he was used to getting picked on because he was small and never quite fit in. In the late 1960s when, even at this age, the kids were experimenting with longer hair, Sammy's father insisted he cut his almost to the skin every two weeks. This only served to accentuate ears that stuck almost straight out.

At first, Sammy tried silencing his detractors with his fists. This strategy usually ended with him flat on his back. Next he practiced the theory that the best defense was a good offense, so he became the aggressor. He had to choose carefully. His victims were those unfortunates that children have picked on since the dawn of time. They were funny looking, had odd habits, not too bright, not good at sports… and in Sammy's case, predominately girls. If Sammy could elicit a laugh from taking a swipe at another kid even less fortunate than he, then that was one day that he didn't need to worry about being the victim again.

In the fifth grade, Sammy just knew his troubles were over. A new girl and her family moved to the area, and this poor girl quickly became the bane and the brunt of the entire class, even without Sammy's help. Her name was Nancy and she was small and pale. She was not physically unattractive, just very plain. The few times she did speak, she was soft-spoken She found it impossible to make any friends. For almost two years she was laughed at, taunted and ridiculed. Her only crime was that she was quiet, and that made her different.

Sammy had a field day. Nancy would take a shock of her hair and tie it in a ponytail and style it so it was situated on the side of her head, not the back. Sammy would pour water on it, dip it in paint, or just play with it when he could get away with it. This attention from him usually ended with Nancy running off in tears and Sammy being sent to the principal's office. It was he who laughed the loudest, and the trips to the office were his badge of courage. On the playground she was like wounded game in the wild. The teacher could not be everywhere at once and Sammy was relentless.

At the end of sixth grade, Sammy and the other children were still not mature enough to realize that Nancy had subjected herself to their torture for two years, yet she never missed a day of school. They were all too young to recognize strength of character. They all graduated and went their separate ways.

In high school Sammy became just another face and he was grateful for the anonymity. After graduation, he could not find a job and did not have the discipline for college, so he joined the Navy. His first stop: Viet Nam. He chose to be a Navy corpsman and was stationed with the Marines. He figured, rightly so, that he would have some viable career choices when he returned home.

He almost never made it. Pinned down in an ambush, he was called upon to care for wounded soldiers. Of necessity, he had to expose himself to the enemy many times. During one of those instances, he made a vow. He knew a Higher Power existed, but he didn't know His name and had no idea how to call on Him. Frankly, until his life was in jeopardy, he could not have cared less. Pinned down and alone, he spoke aloud to himself more than anyone else, swearing that should he make it home alive, he would "right all his wrongs."

An enemy shell creased his skull and he passed out. And he had a dream.

He was back in boot camp. He was in the ring with the pugil sticks – the sticks with wads of padding on either end. He and his opponent were bent on pounding the living daylights out of each other. But he looked, and he saw death in his opponent. He was standing there... as ugly as ugly can get. Sammy wanted to step away but he knew that if he stepped away he would step into a spot where death would put him down. He was hesitant. There was no safer place than flat on your back, on the canvas, with the referee of the universe counting six... seven... eight... you're dead.

But Sammy, for all his faults, was making wise choices. The guy who comes out on top is the guy who embraces death. Show death that you are the one most willing to die.

When he came to, the battle still raged. When it was over, he would not be able to remember what happened. He had pulled five wounded men to safety.

Not only did he survive the firefight, but he made it home a decorated Navy Petty Officer.

To his credit, he never forgot his vow. He lived with his parents, who had since moved to another city. Sammy rented a small room from them, the extra income and his help around the house helping them immensely. He decided to use a portion of his substantial earnings and benefits from the military to go to college. One day he told his mother that there was a task he felt he needed to complete, a wrong he needed to make right. Once accomplished, he explained, his life would be full, no matter what else might lay in store for its remainder.

He told his mother of the girl that he had tormented endlessly in grammar school, the girl named Nancy Burgeson. There had been absolutely no reason for his actions other than he felt tall when he was beating people down. He was going to find her and apologize, and do whatever it took to convey his sincerity to her. College was three months away; he would have plenty of time to search her out.

It proved to be a daunting task. He traveled back to his hometown researching old yearbooks and asking neighbors, those who still lived there and remembered his classmates. The family had moved, but no one knew where or when. He spent his own money chasing down leads. One year later, he was no closer. He spent more time, more money. His college tuition was almost gone. He knew he was getting closer, but he missed her, perhaps by just days. His phone bills grew out of control.

Desiring her forgiveness was his obsession. He felt he could not rest until he met her face-to-face. Well-meaning people tried to dissuade him, telling him his heart was in the right place, but those words were not enough for him.

"God has forgiven you, now forgive yourself and let it go!" But, he could not forgive and forget his misdeeds until she gave him permission to do so. How could he ask anyone or any Higher Entity for forgiveness until she had released him? No. The thorn in his side must be removed before he could ask a god to forgive him.

He never made it to college. He never made it out of his parent's home. They blamed his affliction on the war, but he knew better. He was never a bother and kept up on his rent. Always in the forefront of his mind was Nancy.

With the dawn of the Internet age, his hope and determination grew. He could not hold a job for long because he could not pull himself away from the computer. What made it worse were the questions. What if she was married and changed her name? What if her parents had died? Indeed, the Internet was a blessing, but it was a nightmare as well. A search of the name "Burgeson" returned hundreds of possibilities, scattered all over the nation.

His obsession began to take its toll on his health. He slept fitfully, fewer hours each night. His blood pressure rose. He acquired a bleeding stomach ulcer. His vision was failing. He snacked, but rarely had a good meal. His room was littered with half-open cereal boxes and crackers. He would grab a few boxes of whatever foodstuffs he could get a hold of and, without a word, drive away for several days. Just as suddenly, he would be back, dirty and disheveled.

Death was in the ring. The battle raged all around. The referee was counting. "Six... seven... eight..." and Sammy was on the canvas, content, safe.

His mother entered his room several times one day, only to find him staring at the computer screen, open mouthed and expressionless. Only when she returned the last time and saw that he had not shifted position, did she realize he was dead. The stomach contents, revealed on autopsy, confirmed that the bottle he had in his hand at the time of his death was once filled with potent amphetamines, whipping his body until it could take no more.

It is never easy being a Sammy. It is certainly more difficult than being a Nancy. Strength of character... Is it inherited? Learned? Is there someone to blame here? Did his mother and father dare not discipline?

The torment of unanswered questions literally haunted Sammy to death. Did Nancy become stronger for her suffering? When she left grammar school was she allowed to live a normal life? Did she marry? Did she know what he was going through?

Would Sammy be alive today if he had just been brave enough to forgive himself?

Perhaps in the afterlife, he would look down and see where Nancy got her strength. Just perhaps, Nancy realized at an early age that forgiveness was the most generous virtue that human nature has to offer. Forgiveness means no ulcers. Fewer sleepless nights. The ability to go forward.

Oh, sure. Perhaps Sammy was a coward. Even cowards can do good and heroic deeds, even conquer. But forgive? No. It is not in their nature. The power of doing it flows from a nature possessed by the Nancys of the world; blessed with a soul conscious of its own immortality, and desiring only at the end of the day to seek out and enjoy the perfect rest that only a forgiving God can provide. They sleep and are comforted. In their agony they have not harmed. They ran from their tormentors, but never out of cowardice.

Forgiveness is better than obsession. Rest is better than torment.

Sammy could never rest because he could never forgive himself, even though the Creator forgave him.

*Had the Creator forgiven me? Had I learned to forgive, or am I too late?*

Good night, Nancy Burgesen, wherever you are.

## Chapter 19:
# *Actus Ultimus Orsus Est*
## (The Final Act of The Beginning)

It is late. Michael is alone in his study, reading at his desk under the light of a small lamp. Incredibly, it is a Bible. I smile. He has grown, and that is good, because there is yet an eternity of iniquities to pardon... a lot to be accomplished. I peer over his shoulder. He is reading from the nineteenth chapter of *Luke*. It has always been one of my favorites.

"...He sent two of His disciples, saying, 'Go ye into the village over against you; in the which at your entering ye shall find a colt tied, whereon never a man sat: loose him, and bring him.'

"And if any man ask you, 'Why do ye loose him?' thus shall ye say unto him, 'Because the Master hath need of him.'"
(From the New King James)

Michael is lost in thought. His mind wanders. Sleep begins to overtake him. His eyes are heavy. As he has done so many times, he thinks of Ed, he relives a moment of his life with Adelina. His eyes close, he rests his head on his arms. It is night but he sleeps amidst a soft light.

*Rest in peace, Michael. The Master has need of you.*

# About the Author

Michael Pace has been a registered nurse for over 40 years. He is now a retired Navy Commander who served in Viet Nam, Iran and Iraq during his 28 years of service.

He admits that the most amazing and satisfying job he ever held was his job with the funeral home.

He enjoys restoring old cars and can't seem to stay away from a good cigar. He currently lives in Eugene Oregon with his wife of 34 years along with dogs, cats and a parrot.

To contact Michael Pace or to order additional copies of this book directly from him, send an email to: ixoye333@comcast.net

Made in the USA
Middletown, DE
22 September 2019